Spilled Tea Tastes Better

Kools Bittersweet!!

Spilled Tea Tastes Better

Kools Bittersweet!!

Zelda Ecolia Irby

Spilled Tea Tastes Better! Kools Bittersweet!

Copyright © 2024 by Zelda Ecolia Irby

Printed in the United States of America

ISBN: 979-8-218-58925-7

Published by: Joseph's Ministry, LLC
www.josephsministryllc.com

All rights reserved. This book or any portion thereof may not be reproduced or used in any manner whatsoever without the express written permission of the author except for the use of brief quotations in a book review.

TABLE OF CONTENTS

Dedication……………………………………………………..…7

Acknowledgement………………………………………………...13

Special Thank You……………………………………………..…15

Introduction…………………………………………………........17

Chapter 1: Spilled Tea…………………………………………….35

Chapter 2: I'm a Little Teapot……………………………………65

Chapter 3: Reading the Tea Leaves………………………………83

Chapter 4: Steeped Tea Stirs the Soul…………………………..113

Chapter 5: Beautifully Stained Leaves…………………………..119

Chapter 6: Tea Time……………………………………………..137

Author Bio………………………………………………………161

Appendix………………………………………………………...163

    Be Kind to Animals Too……………………………………163

    My Aunt Frankie and My Great Aunt Janice……………….167

    Pictures……………………………………………………..175

Dedication

I would like to dedicate my first book to my father and my mother. My father, Mr. Henry E. Irby, Sr., who taught me about the golden rules that he was raised with and lived by. Daddy made a determination that his rules would be good enough for me to abide by and live with as well. To this day, I still live by most of the rules and standards that he established for me as a child into my adulthood. As I live and breathe, my dad was my hero, and his spirit remains embedded in my heart, mind, and soul. Before he passed from this world on July 21, 1993, at 2:50 a.m., I had a special event honoring him – "A Famous Black Man" tribute. The tribute took place on my 47th Valentine's birthday. I wanted to do something special for Daddy because I knew that his days on earth were limited due to his illnesses. My art teacher from high school and I stayed in touch years after I graduated, and Mr. Sam Gilliam (RIP) became a world-renowned abstract artist. I called Sam one day and asked if he could refer me to an artist to paint my dad's portrait, and he gave me Simi Knox's name and telephone number. I went to Simi's studio, and I got on his schedule for him to paint Daddy's portrait! It was an amazing process to observe. More importantly, I invited Simi to bring some of his work to my house where I had the special tribute for my dad during my 47th Valentine's birthday celebration. Simi and Daddy met each other face to face. It was such a happy occasion, as Simi got an opportunity to showcase some of his artwork in my house for my friends and family and meet my dad – the man I had commissioned Simi to paint. Unfortunately, Daddy passed from this world before Simi Knox could finish painting Daddy's portrait. In my personal way of memorializing my dad, I had Daddy's portrait displayed beside his coffin at his homegoing service so that family and friends would be able to see the finished portrait for the first time – as it would also be displayed for upcoming family reunions and other special family and local community events. Our relationship as father and daughter was as solid as Mount Kilimanjaro, despite its dormant volcanic cones never erupting. He taught me many lessons. Some of those lessons came to me very easily, as I learned and appreciated them, while other lessons did not sink in so easily because I had to do it my way! My way, in so many experiences, caused me a great deal of unnecessary pain and suffering until I finally accepted that Daddy's rules and standards of teachings were complete acts of love and protection to prevent me from the harshness and cruelties that come with living a good, healthy, and productive life overall. Although he has since passed from this world, so many of his loving and powerful words still ring aloud in my headspace and tug at my heartstrings. They encourage me to always strive to be the best person that I can be and that no other human being is better than me and that I'm not better than anyone else. In most cases, I have come to believe that Daddy was right, despite what others may believe. Daddy, I will miss you FOREVER! Love you, Sassy Mae!

My mother, Mrs. Elizabeth Josephine Irby, was a gorgeous, strong- willed, and independent woman who loved her family. Despite our early relationship being a contentious one, as time went forward, we found ourselves loving and even liking each other more and more. Later on in my life, when I became a mother, I was grateful for my mother and the woman she had become. One day, it dawned on me that Mom was the oldest of eight children – from the Depression generation – in which racism and poverty were mainstream features of American society – as well as the entire world for that matter. I could only imagine when she was growing up, at that time, how hard it must have been to survive all of the hardships. She was also born in the state of Virginia, which back then, was a true and real RED state! But my mother had dreams too. She had goals to meet, and she met them. Having all of us by the time she was 21 years young and working for Uncle Sam back in that area was a major accomplishment! I remember her telling me, one time, about how determined she was to graduate high school, move to the District of Columbia, and get a good government job! Evidence proves that my mother had aspired to fulfill her dreams and reach her goals in life. After she and my dad met at the Pentagon, they fell in love, got married, and had Henry, Jr. (aka Dickie), ME, and Kenny Boy, and we became a family. During brief conversations with my grandmother, she told me stories about how inseparable my parents were and when she saw one of them alone, the other one was not far behind. My mom had class and style. She loved her children, her siblings, her church, and she made sure that her children would become Christians like her and Daddy. Along with my brothers, I was honored and blessed to take care of my mother in her final years before she transitioned to heaven. I realize now, after all of this time, her life must have been hard while growing up with seven other mouths to feed, clothe, and shelter, but she survived it all because she was my mother. So, I learned, over time, that I too can survive all of my challenges before my homegoing (no time soon I pray). I get a lot of my determination and strength traits from my mother. Despite the challenges or difficulties, she would always figure out a path to make life better for herself! Now the element of time has proven to me that courage and pride may skip a generation or two, but it is pleasant when it shows up again in future generations. I love you, Mom. You're my Shero.

Acknowledgement

I would like to acknowledge my one and only living daughter, Allison Elizabeth Irby Vu. Allison Elizabeth Irby Vu, from the day that you were born, you changed my life, for the better. Today, and forever more, you will always be a blessing to me. Please know that you are the one who I waited for and could take care of. I regret, every day of my life, that I did not bring all of my other children into this world, and I believe that my God has forgiven me of my transgression. I love you Allison, Mum.

Chops, thank you for introducing me to Tara. Tara, thank you for writing your book entitled, *When Hope Speaks*, regarding the struggles of motherhood. From your book, I was able to find Meagan Pinkney, an extremely patient and talented individual that I appreciate helping me accomplish another lifelong goal of writing and publishing my first book.

Enzo Alexandra Irby Vu, my grandson, you brought me joy the very first time I ever saw your face. I pray that your life be filled with peace, understanding, less confusion, solid experiences, an enlightening education – including exciting adventures in sports – as you grow and develop. Learn to appreciate these things every day of your life. Just know that ALL experiences have consequences, and I pray that you pick up on the clarity of understanding one major golden rule: Make every effort to treat people like you want to be treated, and remember that a good run is always better than a bad stand any day. Also, as you continue to grow and develop and travel up and down paths with others you meet in this world, try very hard to share less information about yourself with others in order to limit them from treating your kindness and friendship as weakness. Finally, be kind and good to your mother all of the days of your life. She loves you just like I do, and I pray on the daily that our God will let me live long enough to see you become a grown man. Love you, Grand-Zee.

Special Thank You

I would like to thank the following individuals who have contributed to my well-being and my life in a very special way. *Thank you.*

My Godparents, Mr. & Mrs. Milton Bond, thank you for being a part of my journey to this land here on earth. Godfather Milton (RIP), your spirit will forever be with me because you were good to your family, to me and to so many others. Just know that I still have and use the spoon you used to stir food for your crew during your service to this country in the Navy! I use it all of the time.

To my Fairy Godmother, Mrs. Joyce Robinson Bond, I'm so blessed to still have you in my life and to share the good spaces and times we have together. I adore you now and shall always love you because I'm grateful for all of the love and advice you have given me over time, and I am delighted that we still have time to create new memories for others to talk about after both of us have gone back up into the stardust and to be restored by the universe. The heavenly host!

No time soon I pray... Mrs. Mary Valentine Knorl (RIP), who was my 4th, 5th, and 6th grade elementary school teacher at Woodridge Elementary School, and we attended the same church!

You were my first mentor, my friend, mom away from home, and my first culinary guide that exposed me to how to make tuna salad and chocolate chip cookies. I will miss you forever because you were always so kind and good to me as a child.

Dr. George Robert Rhodes (RIP), who was my 7th grade algebra teacher at Taft Jr. At first, it was strange when I learned that Dr. Rhodes would be in my life again. However, later, I appreciated meeting Dr. Rhodes again in the halls of McKinley High School when I discovered he would enhance my educational opportunities moving forward. I consider Dr. Rhodes to be my first male mentor, my friend, dad away from home, and he became my principal at McKinley High Technical School. With all of the people who could have eulogized Dr. Rhodes, at the last hour, I was called upon, and I was privileged to talk about my friend and principal. May God rest the soul of Dr. Rhodes, including the soul of his beloved wife Dr. Doris Rhodes (RIP), whom he adored as they were true lovebirds into eternity!

Introduction

In October 1980, I returned to work with a promotion to another agency within the same department, after I had been on maternity leave since the end of July. I met the man of my dreams, and my life would never be the same. This is just one spilled tea story in my life that I will share with you in my first book. As you read through my stained tea leaves from my past, you too will come to learn that spilled tea actually does taste better, and it sometimes can be bittersweet. Sometimes in my life, I found that making revisions can be time well spent. To conserve energy in some cases, some individuals may believe that a setback is something negative. However, I have discovered that a setback can be a new beginning! Simply, a fresh start, and another opportunity to finally meet your mark and feel good about your journey moving forward. Despite this, I too have learned that living is a challenge on a daily basis. Sometimes, it is sour and harsh, but at other times, it can also be bittersweet. Heck, my nightmare had only just begun! I had to pinch myself to see if I was still asleep, if I had died, or if I simply had gone straight to hell without a warning!

After having Allison and returning to work, I was about to embark on a new job adventure that came with a promotion, an office, and a clerk for typing assistance if needed. I had always prepared and planned to move upward and forward in my good government career opportunities. I just didn't expect to be getting a promotion while I was on maternity leave. It was in early October 1980. I had to collect my belongings from my previous office and clear out my desk. Despite this, my then supervisor was not happy that I had even accepted and taken the job with a promotion to another agency. I greeted everyone, cleared out my desk and went on my merry way because I was moving on up to the East Side like George and Weezy! Y'all remember *The Jeffersons*, one of Norman Lear's spin-offs from *All in the Family*!

One of the saddest days of climbing my career ladder happened after being promoted twice – including one time after the RIF (Reduction in Force) – and after my second failed marriage. On occasion, I would have to travel to another office building to make presentations about changes in the Equal Employment Opportunity (EEO) regulations or WHATEVER was happening at the time. Soon after being promoted to management, I had to go to the Hyattsville office to make my first presentation to the executives of my agency and Bureau leadership and demonstrate that I knew my job! I was disheartened when two of the highest-ranking Black executives on our team mocked me after my failed marriage, and point blank asked me, "Oh, by the way, are you Mrs. King or Queen?" I was preparing to make one of the most important presentations of my then career to the executives of my agency! These executive clowns definitely hurt my feelings and truly embarrassed themselves in front of their colleagues. I stepped away from the two clowns, went into the ladies' room, splashed my face with some cool water and returned to the room. After I made my outstanding presentation to the executive team of the agency in my Bureau, Clowns Number One and Two worked their way over to me, and I had the privilege to politely dismiss them because my Director, and our then administrator, waved a BIG high-five for me to come over and congratulated me on an excellent performance of my first presentation and thought that I should get an award. So, here's another spilled tea moment for you! Believe it or not, I received the Administrator's Award that year for outstanding service as a public health service worker in government at the department for an outstanding job!

Fortunately, I knew all of the employees in the office where I had gotten the new job, with the exception of the new Director, who had been hired from another agency outside of the department. Some insiders and current personnel weren't happy about their new boss. I had only just gotten there myself, and only time would tell with assignments, other duties as assigned, workload, etc., what my next move would be. I got up from my desk to go get a cup of coffee in the outer office area, and in walks a fine and handsome man into the open bay area of the office looking for me. When I first laid eyes on him, I thought to myself, "DAMN, he's fine." Then I collected myself and kept my knees from buckling. I was able to stand like normal and find out why he wanted to see me. When he called me by name a second time, I heard him loud and clear. The office secretary nudged me with her elbow and confirmed that he was on my calendar for a meeting that day. From that day forward, my life changed drastically! Our organization had meetings for anything and everything. Because I was not the shy type and forever having something to contribute, I found myself in more meetings than I really cared to be in. That was how "other duties as assigned" would get assigned to YOU – like it or not! Underlings who disagreed with that idea of team building would later find themselves labeled as non-team players in their career, which would negatively impact their ongoing good government career.

Back in the day, 1975 to be exact, a small group of public health service workers formed an organization in the federal workforce, called "Blacks in Government" (BIG). It was an up and coming organization that would attract lots of black employees throughout the federal sector, get the attention of corporate America, and forever modify programs under the Equal Employment Opportunity Office nationwide. The announcement of BIG was HUGE NEWS then because everyone who thought he or she had any power was interested in becoming a member. Any black individual who was involved in EEO programs would eventually find a path to get involved with BIG in some form or another. To this day, BIG still conducts its annual conference to help support state and local training programs for youth, economic empowerment, including the creation of political and cultural sites in surrounding communities throughout the country.

To my knowledge, the membership continues to grow. Shortly after BIG became an organization, most of us who were in EEO jobs became members immediately and got involved in the mission of BIG to promote and increase equal employment opportunities for minorities and women, small businesses, recruitment and retention of workers with a discipline in public health (i.e. commissioned corps officers). Being involved in BIG in any form or another was a BIG DEAL then. Like so many organizations, over a period of time, however, organizations can either lose their luster, significance, value, or members due to the current climate.

Now, it's springtime and Allison's growing like a sunflower, and I am enjoying my new job because I have been promoted again, with a Reduction In Force (RIF) government action coming down the pike. Aging employees with many years of service were not upset about the RIF activities because so many of them were eligible to retire, while younger employees were extremely concerned. They had a limited amount of tenure, so it was a simple and easy process to eliminate personnel. Simply put, last hired, first fired is so common in most workplace settings. The talk in the hallways about who would be getting a "PINK SHEET" was as thick as margarine. You could cut it with a knife. I would see employees lined up outside in the hallway to talk with any of us who were not already talking to another employee about the identical RIF concerns. By now, Brother FINE had asked me out for coffee, and I was thrilled because I really liked him. I knew that he already liked me because the child that I had just delivered to earth six months prior to ever meeting him was not his flesh or blood! Once again, I knew that God had blessed me this time around with a decent man who would love and respect me, as I was ready to embrace my happily ever after. Several weeks and months had passed, and we had been dating BIG TIME and enjoying each other's company, meeting family, and sharing friendships! One Sunday, we had gone to church and afterwards, he simply popped the question! "Will you marry me?" I was not at all shocked because I knew that he was in love with me, and I was deeply in love with him. We stopped by my dad's house, and he asked my father. Daddy said, "When did all of this happen?" We left my dad's house and went back to my apartment, had something to eat, I put Allison in her crib for a nap, and I called my mother to tell her the good news. Mom lived too far away for us to do a drop-in without a phone call to her to see if she was home. I called my mother to tell her that I was getting married, and she said, "I'm so glad and happy for you, and I really like this guy. He's got manners, and I like the way he treats you and Allison." We only lived like six blocks from each other, so we saw each other all of the time. Plus, we worked in the same building. Our journey of getting married was on the horizon, and I was as excited as I could be and moved into full mode of planning our wedding – and what a wedding it was. After all of the excitement over the weekend with announcing to our parents that we were going to get married, it's Monday morning, and we are back to work. Before lunch time, the news about our engagement had filled the hallways and cafeteria of the Parklawn building, and my friends and staffers were popping in and out of my office. I went down to the Drug Fair counter where I would get my daily coffee and breakfast to tell Connie and her staff about my engagement, and she and her team were jumping for joy for me and him as well. We moved into the stage of attending weekly marriage counseling sessions to talk with Father West (RIP) and my pastor. We covered everything under the sun, from A to Z, with the exception of what he held back and kept close to his vest and hidden away from me. I was confident that my life was about to change for the better.

The time came to meet his family and get my engagement ring. We had several engagement parties – one at my mom's house on Clark Street, and two in Louisiana (one in New Orleans and the other in Baton Rouge)! His entire family, including his grandmother, mother, step- mother, sisters, and brother were all so kind, gracious, and extremely generous to me and my daughter during our brief and only visit to their homes in Louisiana. Although he had proposed to me early on, I did not actually receive my engagement ring until we got to his stepmom's and dad's home in Baton Rouge. When I first saw my ring, I could not believe my eyes because it was so sparkly, darkly, gorgeous, and heavy too! All of the engagement parties were fabulous. Lots of Louisiana cuisine, everything from crawfish etouffee to delicious gumbo, pecan and praline pies, homemade breads, including that strong BLACK ass coffee which kept me awake for 72 hours. He told me on several occasions that the women in his family were BIG coffee drinkers and that I needed to be mindful of my consumption of caffeine because it would keep me awake. We got back home to

Washington, D. C., and plans for our wedding were underway. We made a pact with each other to not go overboard spending too much money on the wedding because we wanted to buy a home. Buying property was important, so we made a budget, and of course, I did not stick to it. I went over to see Mrs. Val- Jean Mathis (RIP), a seamstress and my neighbor who lived across the street from where I grew up, to discuss making my wedding gown and bridesmaid dresses. I was so happy when Mrs. Mathis said that she would make my dress and the bridesmaids dresses. We met the staff at Richmond's Wedding Salon and made our arrangements for our reception. The place was simply spacious and with each one of us having 250 invitees, we needed a large place to accommodate our guests. We tried, on several different occasions, to cut the number of guests in half, but it just did not happen because we both had a big family with lots of friends. So, we sent out 500 invitations and ended up with 1,200 or so guests at our reception. Of course, we ran out of food and drink. As I recall, all the guests had a great time! When we left the reception hall, we went around the corner to his house and celebrated the wedding that we had just had with a small group of family and a few friends who had come in from out of town. It was a day in my life that I shall never forget because it was so wonderful and filled with love, peace, joy, and forever was on my mind! GIRLS & BOYS, I WAS DEAD WRONG!

He was still bringing his stuff from his house to our apartment. Keep in mind, we are two weeks into our marriage. It's a Friday, and he calls to tell me that he'll be late because he and T-man have an appointment to talk with a lawyer about the house and other stuff because his buddy, T-man, is talking about getting married too. Once again, I am getting excited because we have friends who are getting ready to get married as well. Another week goes by and it's Friday again. This time, I got a call from my then father-in-law who called often to check in to see how "things" were going with us as newlyweds, and I enjoyed hearing from my new in-laws because they were nice people. Our telephone conversations were generally brief because most of the time when my then father-in-law would call, he really wanted to talk with his son. However, during this particular telephone conversation, everything was going well until he reminded me again that he and his family were happy that I had accepted his son for who he is. This time around during our conversation, I paused. I believe I asked him to please explain to me what he meant and why he kept praising me for loving his son so much! In my mind, I was supposed to love him for who he was. He was the man of my dreams, and I felt blessed to have him as a loving husband and a kind person to my daughter, who was not his child. Readers, do me a favor! Buckle up if you like or simply put on a pair of leather gloves because this tea that I am about to spill is going to BURN. It certainly scalded me years ago, but my scars have finally healed over time. PRAISE THE LORD! I would not have been able to do it without believing in GOD! I believed in HIS power of healing, and I had to trust that I would survive, exhale, live and enjoy life again. Pop "K" said to his wife, "Babe, you need to pick up the phone. Zelda's on the line, and we need to talk with her because it's time." Now, I am absolutely confused. I said, "Pop, what's going on?" I hear my then step-mother-in-law's voice when she calls my name and says, "Hello darling, how are you?" I told her that I wasn't sure. I greeted her, and then I began to melt all the way down like a popsicle on a hot day in August, while listening to what his father said and his stepmom confirmed about their son and his life experiences being with T-man and other males – and how grateful they were to me for accepting him for who he was. As I recall, it was a Friday, and I had not yet even consumed my first weekend glass of chardonnay! After I caught my breath, I found my way back up to the sofa from the floor. I exhaled several times, and I told my in-laws that I had to go because I was looking around to see where Allison was in her walker. I was now beginning to boo-hoo and lose myself after hearing what my then in-laws had confessed to me about their beloved son and his best friend. I knew that I had to hang on because I had to take care of my seven month old young daughter. Believe it or not, I heard him turning the key in the door, and then I knew that I was in trouble. With all that, I tried my best to be calm, but I could not. I told him about the telephone conversation that I had just had with his parents. His response was simply, "You called my parents?" I said, "No, your dad called here looking for you." As our conversation progressed, I asked him about his relationship with T-man, and he went ballistic. I followed his lead and bum-rushed him all the way down the hallway with his back up against the T-bar of the window. Had it been open, both of us would have gone down three stories to the ground. Anger brings strength to those in need, and I certainly needed it that day in order to survive the plight of betrayal that I had encountered! I was so exhausted when he left, and I was so glad that he was gone from what I knew as mine and Allison's safe space. I picked up the phone from the floor and called Father West and told him what had just happened, and he told me to come to the church immediately. It remains a blur to me today how fast I picked up Allison, got her into the car seat and headed over to Calvary, 820 "6" Street, N.E. to see Father West. He was waiting for me at the door and took Allison from my arms, and we went into his office. I was boo-hooing and totally out of control and started to tremble. Father West still had Allison in his arms, and he said, "Let's go over into the nave of the church, and I want you to let it all go when we get there." Just know that when I got over to the nave of the church where I was confirmed, sang in the choir, practiced Christianity in general, and had gotten married, I let it GO! God heard me screaming out loud and crying like a baby. Father West kept saying, "Just let it all out," and I screamed for hours. As I write this from memory, my eyeglasses are fogging up right now with tears dropping like rain from a hurricane. Some painful experiences never disappear, but you MUST learn how to live with them and move on.

We are finally back in Silver Spring, on Hewitt Ave., in our apartment, and I knew that I would have to make arrangements to get out and find another place to live. I did not hesitate because I am not that kind of "GIRL!" I found another place for me and Allison to live back in Washington, D.C., on Luzon Avenue, N.W. Here I was catching my breath and repositioning myself once again. When I told my parents, family, and friends that my marriage was over and why, they just couldn't believe it either. I will always remember someone saying, "You just got married, and it hasn't been a month." I was more confused as my heart, mind, and dreams were torpedoed! So, I knew that I needed to talk with a professional who would help me get back on track because my world was completely foggy. Allison, however, was my grace of light and peace through the love of God, as I went through this awful time of my life. Come on now, the reality is that I was climbing the ladder of success in my good government career, I challenged myself to finish my last semester and finally get my degree, I got married to the man who I believed to be the best male I had ever met on God's planet earth, and he turned out to be in love with another

MAN! YES! For the first time in my life, I was devastated and pissed off at the same time because I knew within my being, this could not be happening to ME! Swallowing a piece of broken glass would have been easier to digest. After praying with Father West, day in and day out, I coupled my counseling with an appointment with a psychiatrist who would help me move forward and work through this ordeal because I realized that I was in an uncharted course. I needed assistance to come out on the other side feeling good and being mentally healthy again! TO GOD BE THE GLORY! After six months of therapy, daily and ongoing prayers, being creative, developing new friendships, trusting myself to take time out for self when necessary, learning how to accept consequences, watching my beautimous daughter grow and develop, and knowing that God will never leave me NO MATTER THE CIRCUMSTANCES, I exhaled because the fog had lifted. I could see clearly. My heart and mind were no longer racing against each other. I didn't feel ashamed or like I had done something wrong because I had a plan of action to move forward. I even told Dr. P. to enjoy the rest of his life, and when he needed assistance, to go get it! Fortunately, for me, I learned that love is so profound, and when you love a human being, you just DO! I just wished my husband would have been honest with me because I would have loved him anyway, and we could have just been friends. Like me, most of you who are reading my book know that BETRAYAL is awful because it triggers the lost emotional connection and stability that any relationship brings or suggests. Google the definition. Just know the emotional upset and pain it leaves can be enduring or sometimes last a lifetime. As a REMINDER, YOU MUST LEARN TO LIVE WITH IT AND MOVE ON! Another method is to limit the aftermath. LET IT GO! Believe and know that it is never alright to allow any other human being or thing to pocket or steal your joy! NOT EVER!! I have lived long enough, surviving the damages and destruction betrayal brings to the human spirit in a relationship. I encourage you to know and believe through your own positive energy source of God, that reaching up high and snatching down your power from your heart to FORGIVE any individual who has misled you, lied to you, and or hurt you can be less bitter than you holding on to the betrayal.

Chapter 1
Spilled Tea

So much to tell...

Where it All Began

While walking my dog, Sir Tobi, one foggy morning, I had an epiphany! It was so strong!! Simply put, I realized at that particular moment that I owed a lot of gratitude to my mother, grandmother, great grandmother, my Fairy Godmother and Mom, Nettie Herbert, my aunts, Mrs. Mary Valentine Knorl, (RIP) (4th, 5th, 6th grade teacher), and all of the women who have been in my life from the time I was born. I learned that despite whatever I thought I wanted at that time and just had to have, these women always had my best interest at heart and shielded me from myself. This was to all help prevent me from tripping, falling, and hitting rock bottom as I was growing and developing into a human being. Some folks might refer to people with these unique positive qualities of loving and caring as "Guardian Angels". Writing this book has allowed me to appreciate that spilling my own tea is not an accident! Nothing at all like knocking over a hot cup of tea from a pot!

It is not one of those types of tea spills. Rather, these are real life and time experiences that either I have encountered or someone close to me, and they have allowed me to share their stories. I will not share their real names in order to protect the innocent or the ones who have passed on to Glory to be with the heavenly host. But there are a few of my friends who are allowing me to use their real names, as our friendships are lifelong – all the way to the grave. The time has finally come, and now I can share some of my stories and experiences with you. Just know that I am spilling my tea with you on purpose, and hopefully, at some point, as you keep reading, you will be happy that you selected my first book to read. I hope that you will come to the conclusion that you had another unique reading experience because I gave you a window into my life in the absence of you looking right into my eyes to take a peek at my soul. I want to share with you the type of person I am, yet know I will reposition myself whenever I find the need to do so. Time, relationships, general life experiences, including traveling to other countries and seeing how others live, have taught me that regardless of where you were born on the globe, upon your awakening, living is an everyday challenge. At the same time, be able to understand and appreciate that each one of us are a gift to each other from the grace and love of God.

    I hope you enjoy my spilled tea moments because I believe if you have a network at home, at work, or in your surrounding community that it is wide and long enough for you to tap into. Whenever you need help and support to serve you or to reach your goals, use it. Nonetheless, I consider it a blessing period! It too proves that you're not alone in this world. If you will allow me to reflect from days gone by in one of the TV commercials featuring Michael Jordan, stating, "Be Like Mike." Like so many, I sang Mike's praises a couple times myself. But another entire age has come and gone! Believe it or not, as you keep reading my book, we are living in the age of "AQUARIUS," which just happens to be my zodiac sign. Imagine that. Not bragging or boasting by any means. Since God lives in each and every one of us, I encourage you to embrace His love, peace, and joy, and discover your own joy and strength. I could stress that you try something entirely unique and different, so I strongly suggest you be like me. Simply put, if spilling your own tea helps lift your spirits and helps you feel good about yourself, then go on and do it because it is your tea to spill. Who knows? You may inspire or encourage someone along the way, as so many men and women have inspired me. I am now a joyful ole young woman at the tender age of 78 by the time you read my first book. That's a blessing!!! Be mindful, as human beings, I believe that we all have a dark side. I am one of those individuals who makes every effort to keep my double midnight dark blue side mixed with other colors of my emotions and feelings so that I can avoid having dull moments and days of misunderstandings with others, while I continue living my best life God has blessed me with. As I believe, that when you love your mind, you persevere, as the brain is not an English muffin with all its nooks and crannies waiting to be smeared with butter and a heaping teaspoon of marmalade.

My Family

Despite everything, I am the little teapot born to parents who came from extremely humble beginnings. To be born during the Depression generation, to later meet and become husband and wife despite the economy crashing, what a moment! Under this cloud of wreckage, I learned that people fall in love regardless of what is happening around them. Believe it or not, I remember when I was a little teapot, steaming all over the place here and there, trying to find my way and make a space in this world for myself, my grandmother told me that my parents were inseparable. And then me and my brothers were born.

My parents worked awfully hard for me and my brothers. Both of them were born in the southern part of the United States. Daddy was born in Greenville, South Carolina, the youngest of 10 siblings. My mom was born in Virginia, the oldest of eight. While this may not be a hot spill of tea at the moment – it was in the spring, the birds were singing, and it began to look fresh outside of our apartment window. There were tree-lined streets and green healthy grass and pretty flowers popping up everywhere, including across the street from Mrs. Lockhart's yard.

It was May. Me, my brothers, and other children who attended Logos Nursery school, located at 700 6th Street, N.E. Washington, would participate in the annual event to wrap the May Pole. This annual event was a big deal back in the day, and Mom would tell Daddy that she would be going downtown on "F" Street, to purchase our clothing outfits from the Esther Shop and pick up our shoes from Boyce and Lewis. The "May Day" event was so special back in the day. We would get all dressed up in ALL white from head to toe and wrap that pole, even as we ran into each other and fell to the ground. Because this was a major event in the community, my mom would only have it one way! Simply put, her children would be dressed to the nines for the occasion and looking good for the celebration. Of course, at the tender age of 5 or 6 years, we didn't have a clue about what it meant to be dressed to the nines, but my mom certainly knew, as Daddy stood over by the fence and looked on as his children and other kids were photographed by the head of our nursery school, Mr. Christian (RIP). That special event of wrapping that May Pole has been enshrined in my memories and will be for years to come. Although our apartment was small, Daddy's father stayed with us for a spell. Through reading tea leaves here and there and everywhere, I learned that our first and original babysitter was our second cousin, Mrs. Jean Robinson White, who just turned 90 years young this past March 12, 2024. The celebration her children had for her was simply a hot tea moment and human beings at any age could appreciate it!

Our Grandpa John was a soft-spoken man but extremely demanding when he wanted something done. I am convinced that some of his demands may have been the cause of his visit with us to be cut short. Shortly thereafter Grandpa John left our apartment, Aunt Frankie (RIP) came to stay with us for a short time as she attended Cardozo High School. The purpose of her staying with us was to help look after us as our parents worked and attended school. But her visit with us was short- lived, and she went back home across the "14" Street Bridge. Later, Mrs. Lockhart (RIP), who lived across the street from us, kept an eye on us, and soon after we simply became latchkey kids.

We were so blessed back in the day to have so many loving

family members who could help look after us when we were children, as there were five living generations. As we lived and got older, some of us were truly blessed to see five living generations for a second time in our lifetime, with my mother being photographed in both pictures that were taken to celebrate and capture both milestones, in 1968 and 2017. Unlike some children, we were also blessed to go and stay with either aunts and uncles – great or even great great – at the end of school closing for summer. That's how large our family was. After Aunt Frankie went back home, and school closed for the summer, me and my brothers were separated from each other for the entire summer season, and we stayed with other aunts and uncles until school opened again in the fall. I would go stay with Great Aunt Janice and Uncle Palmer at 412 "H" Street, N.E., Washington, D.C. Kenny Boy would go to stay with Great Aunt Norma in Barry Farm, S.E., and my oldest brother, Henry Jr., named after our father and better known as Dickie, would go to our grandparents' house in Arlington, Virginia.

As we got older, during the spring and summer months, my oldest brother would serve papers, cut folks' lawns, and shovel snow during the winter to earn extra cash. I earned extra money by ironing my Daddy's white shirts, at $.25 per shirt, and I took on odd jobs with the more affluent neighbors in my "hood" at the time. Every Saturday, I would go to Ms. McDonald's house to wash her dishes, iron her napkins, tablecloths, sheets, pillowcases, and run the vacuum. She paid me very well, so I always had a few extra bucks in my pocket to buy another pair of 19-teens because my parents made it very clear that neither one of them would ever spend $19 to buy me a half of a shoe, and if I wanted a pair, I would have to work to buy them. So, I did! I had several pairs too! Ms. McDonald recommended me to some of her friends – in particular, a couple who lived around the corner. Now, I had two jobs, and I could earn money to get extra items that I wanted without having to ask Mom or Dad. Once I finished my job at Ms. McDonald's house, I would go around the corner and work for Mr. George and Mrs. Ann Moore, who lived in what we used to call the "Hansel and Gretel" house. They recommended me for my first BIG babysitting job to babysit the first-born son of Dr. LaSalle D. Leffall Jr. (RIP). He was an excellent physician and good human being. I had an excellent reputation taking care of people even when I was a youngster. It always made me feel good to know that older people trusted and recommended employment opportunities for me at such a young age. Later, I was honored by my art teacher Mr. Sam and Mrs. Dorothy Gilliam to babysit their first-born daughter.

Aunt Janice and Uncle Palmer (RIP)

One of my most exciting and interesting jobs was when I visited and stayed with my Aunt Janice and Uncle Palmer. I was helping them with greeting families who lost their loved ones through death. My Aunt and Uncle were morticians. I was so awfully young – 6 or 7 – at the time, and for whatever reason, I was not afraid of being around dead people or people who worked in that industry. My brothers and cousins were true scaredy cats. Generally, whenever Aunt Janice was downstairs working in her office, I would sometimes be napping on the other side in the showroom where the caskets were on full display for family members to make their selection as they grieved the loss of their loved one. Simply put, tea is not always meant for two. On one particular morning while Aunt Janice and Uncle

Palmer were upstairs meeting to make arrangements with a family, I noticed the heavy double doors were open. Mr. Pickett (embalmer) was not on site, so I decided to step in and take a look around like I had done so many times before. Unfortunately, my foot hit the stopper that was holding the door open and caused both doors to close. So, I pressed down on the large bar to open the door. It did not open, and that is when I realized I was locked on the inside of the morgue with six bodies, and I would not be able to get out until either Mr. Pickett returned or Aunt Janice or Uncle Palmer missed me. Several hours had passed and no one popped in. Then all of a sudden, there was Aunt Janice shouting, "Here she is Palmer, locked inside the morgue." As much as Aunt Janice loved me, she scolded me real good again about playing around on this side of the building without her knowledge or adult supervision. This time, I was really nervous because I had never been locked in a room and that close to that many dead bodies without an adult being around. Whew!! After I was rescued, Mr. Pickett went home, and Aunt Janice and Uncle Palmer and I went back upstairs to have the delicious chicken and dumplings Aunt Janice had prepared earlier that morning for our late supper. I guess I was used to being around dead people because Aunt Janice and Uncle Palmer told me that dead people will never hurt you. It's the live ones that I should be concerned about. Believe it or not, I had aspired to become a mortician. I didn't achieve that goal because my Uncle Palmer died in the early 60s, when "Sherry" by Frankie Valli and Four Seasons was a hit record. My late, beloved and darling Great Aunt Janice lost the business after Uncle Palmer died because she could not manage the business anymore by herself. His death took a toll on her. Her beloved husband and director of Mr. L.P. Palmer, of Palmer Funeral Home, 412 "H" Street, Northeast Washington, D.C had passed this life and left her behind. It later became Washington Funeral Home, and my darling Great Aunt Janice left the city and moved to Virginia, where she stayed with her brother until her death in 1977. I still miss her charm, classy style, creative energy, and loving ways. She was such a good human being. She adored me, and I her! For the rest of my life, I will always miss my Great Aunt Janice and Uncle Palmer. I ADORED THEM!

My Dad

My dad was a champion as a father. He was my hero, and I was his only daughter that he nicknamed Sassy Mae. Whenever he called me Zelda, I knew that I was in trouble. The only other person in the family who called me Sassy Mae, is my darling cousin, Mrs. Jean Robinson White. Daddy was a hardworking man who was born and raised in Greenville, South Carolina, with nine other siblings, lots of nieces and nephews – including twin nephews – and lots of cousins. Most of the time, Daddy worked two extra jobs, including his own business as a painter, in brick masonry, and as a plasterer. He created a plaster "SWIRL" that is unmatched to any other plaster design I have ever seen to this day. As a matter of fact, I remember the mayor from Glass Manor calling our house on a regular basis because people in the industry liked Daddy's "SWIRL" design. It had become popular in the DMV (District of Columbia, Maryland, and Virginia). Our kitchen phone would be ringing off the hook. Whenever the caller was trying to reach my father, I would take a message and later call Daddy at the Gulf Service Station on "H" Street where he was working his part time job, to let him know that the mayor of Glass Manor wanted a callback because he had gotten another request for Daddy to do his famous "SWIRL" on a wall out there somewhere.

On the weekends, it was hard for any of us to talk on the telephone to our friends and have a good conversation because most of the phone calls were requests for Daddy to work. That's what happens when you're a master plasterer! You rarely even hear the word *plasterer* anymore because so much construction inside housing is drywall now. I remember at Christmas time, Daddy would be working at Mr. Love's hardware store on "H" Street. I recall Mr. Love being a very nice man, but Jasper White, at the Gulf Station, was not always so pleasant. Unlike Jasper White, Mr. Sam Delisi was an extremely nice person and a good friend to my dad. When Mr. Delise passed from this world, Daddy took in his two German shepherds, Duke and Duchess, and my father was not that fond of animals until he met me. I remember Daddy telling me that after he came to Washington after leaving Greenville, one of his first jobs was as a short order cook somewhere off Benning Road. Although Daddy worked all sorts of jobs to earn money and survive, I feel good that I can attribute some of my Jill of all Trades to some of the skill sets I got from my dad. His influence over me from the time I was a child was strong because we talked about everything all of the time. Our kitchen countertop talks were the best because it was my favorite seat in the house whenever Daddy provided any of his many lectures to me. I didn't like that seat, however, whenever he was telling me to go get a switch to punish me with a spanking. He gave me nine hits in my entire life! Most of the time, I got out of being hit because I would start screaming, and he didn't want the neighbors to hear! Yes! I was a DADDY'S GIRL! Keep reading! As you turn the pages, you'll discover some spilled tea moments that are hot and some not so much, but *kool* to understand. Daddy shared the importance of participating in the political process of voting, serving others, being a good Christian, respecting self and others, and understanding that a good run is always better than a bad stand. I used to love being outside most of the time because I felt free!

Back in the day, most children played outside until the streetlights came on, and you simply went in the house. Because you did not want your mom or dad coming to the front door and screaming out your name in front of your friends saying, "Get your butts in this house." Some parents expressed themselves differently by walking down the steps onto the sidewalk to escort their children back inside, but that never happened to me because I knew better. As I grew up, I began to challenge both my parents by asking lots of questions. I was one of those children who had many questions. Sometimes I was successful getting the answer that I thought that I wanted to hear, and when I didn't get the answer that I wanted to hear, I would just keep asking until it led to me being punished. I hated being scolded. Even after I got the answer, I would challenge the answer with another *WHY*? Later, I learned to sometimes draw my own conclusions, which led me to begin to suffer because I was flexing my wings – or as my grandmother would say, "You're beginning to smell yourself." But I knew that it was time to check myself because I did not want to take that awful and threatening slap in the face or land out there somewhere in a place called, "Oblivion." Being the only girl and being raised with two brothers, I always felt secure and safe because of our daily conversations with Daddy and sometimes with Mom as well. I believe that Daddy was teaching me how to take care of myself, inside and outside of the house, as I was gearing up to step out onto the world stage of LIFE! I will spill more tea about this specific phase of my life as you read on.

My father loved my mother and his children. I remember my grandmother telling me several times that Mom and Dad were inseparable, and she told me about how much they loved each other. My daddy worked hard for us to ensure that we had everything that we needed, and sometimes, we even got extra items that we dreamed about having, like my purple English racer. I still have sweet memories about my Valentine's Day birthdays, Christmases, and other holidays in general when we lived in our apartment at 315 "G" Street – where Mrs. Louise Lockhart, who lived across the street from us, kept a watchful eye on us when Mom and Dad were at work. We were really young during this part of my journey, like age 4 or 5. My memory remains pretty crisp and fresh today because I can still recall so much from the days of 315 "G" Street, until we moved into the house on 26th Street, and beyond. Annually, in late October or early November, my daddy would climb the pear tree in our backyard with that sack on his back to harvest the fruit and share them with the greatest cooks in our family. After he picked the pears, he would fill the boxes and deliver the freshly picked pears to his sisters and my Great Aunt Janice. On occasion, we would drive all the way down to the country to take some pears to my great aunts, Great Great Aunt Dovey, grandmother, and great grandmother. This is where my aunts and grandmother would jumpstart their pickling and preserving of fruits and veggies to be stored for the upcoming seasons. Some of the fruit and veggie jars were gifted to friends and family at holiday time. The steps involved in the pickling and preserving of fruits and veggies is a BIG ORDEAL! I watched the women in my family pickle and preserve fruits and veggies year after year, season after season. Today, although I have tried many times, I still cannot – for the life of me – pickle or preserve fruits and veggies. I recall that when Thanksgiving, Christmas, and Easter time came around, that they used to exchange their jars of fruits and veggies with each other and give them away to friends and other family members. I can still smell the cloves, the nutmeg, the cinnamon, and the juices that came from the jars once opened.

      When I knew I was in trouble with Mom or a teacher, I always felt safe at night after Daddy got home from work with his clothing covered in paint and plaster because no matter what time he came in, he would always kiss me on my forehead and ask me if I was alright. Then I would fall asleep. I remember the time when Daddy and I fell out because he found my black and white composition books that I used to write in. I would tie them up with a ribbon once I completed a booklet and put it in a box under my bed. One day, I went to write, and my books were GONE! Shortly after our conversation, I stopped writing because I felt BETRAYED and knew that Daddy now knew all of my secrets. I really had not done anything bad or wrong yet, to my knowledge, but Dad and I would NOT EVER speak about my books again. I believe within my heart and spirit that he did not find anything bad enough to bring to my attention. If he had, I am sure we would have had many more conversations to follow. Daddy was the baby of 10 siblings. His oldest sister had 14 children, and according to family reunion stories, Aunt Bert (RIP) raised seven other children who were not her own. My Aunt Bert loved and adored my father, her baby brother, and his nephews loved him. They would drive their mother up from Greenville to see Daddy whenever she wanted to visit him.

Most of my aunts from my daddy's side of the family

migrated North like he did and lived within communities close to each other. So, getting to know my aunts, my uncles by marriage, and my cousins was fun and easy. I enjoyed being around my aunts because they were always cooking something. I attribute some of my culinary skills today to yesterday's recipes, as well as to me paying attention to measuring certain seasonings for an exciting culinary experience – with the exception of pickling and preserving fruits and veggies. My aunts loved their baby brother, and he and I partook of the delicious meals every time we visited any one of his three beloved sisters who lived close by. My father was a proud 33rd degree Mason. When I would ask him questions about why he wore the ring all of the time, he shared that it was pride and an element of service. I would ask him questions about his meetings, but he would tell me nothing about his meetings. He would tell me to stop asking him because the information he obtained from his lodge meetings were secret and none of my business. As time went by, I stopped asking because he would never say anything. Daddy was a Baptist and Mom was an Episcopalian. As I remember, going to church on Sundays was difficult in our household because Mom wanted us to go to her church and Daddy wanted us to go to church with him. Well, just know, that me and my brothers grew up and were raised as Episcopalians. I remember one Saturday before we were getting ready to go to church for choir rehearsal, that my brothers were playing next door in Michael Borky's driveway. I decided to join them like most times. All they were doing were running up the driveway and jumping forward onto the T-bar of the clothesline and turning themselves over the bar. I watched them turn themselves over several times, and now it was my turn to show them up and brag that I could do it too! I turned over around the T-bar a couple times, and then I decided to stand up and walk the clothesline itself! My youngest brother, Kenny Boy, started hollering out, "Mom, Zelda's hurt and her arm looks really funny looking." In a heartbeat, I fell and broke my arm in three places. I couldn't get up right away because my right hand was now located on the other side of my body. YIKES! Mom rushed me to the hospital, and I was in a heavy cast for six months. I was only in the third grade, nine years old, and now faced with having to write with my left hand because I had broken my right arm. This reminded me of another accident that I had while growing up when I was staying with Aunt Janice and Uncle Palmer during the summer. My next-door neighbor, Julie, and I used to play on a rooftop where there were skylights. One day, we were playing outside on the roof, and Julie was much heavier than me. After she slid down the skylight, she cracked the glass, but I did not know it was cracked. When it was my turn to slide down the skylight, my buttocks discovered the crack, a piece of glass had broken off, and I was caught and trapped in the skylight. Julie looked over at me and waved saying, "I'll see you later." I looked around, and there she was climbing back into the window. I am thinking that someone would be coming out to rescue me and no one ever came. I started screaming for help! I began to think, *"Damn, I am stuck outside in the skylight and bleeding."* After what felt like forever, my aunt heard me, and she and Uncle Palmer came out on the roof and took me to Rogers Memorial Hospital for care. As I recall, the attending doctor tricked me and told me to close my eyes. When I opened them, I saw a mask coming down on my face and I was out. When I woke up, I had stitches and then we went back home. Julie was punished for leaving me outside and not telling anyone that I was outside, and we never spoke again afterwards. Now I am 10 years old.

My Brothers

Spilling tea can be a good thing in our society today despite the notion that some folks believe social media has the monopoly on what's up! Well, I beg to differ because spilling the "NEWS" on what's happening now doesn't always have to be something negative! I know that to be a fact because I am blessed with brothers, and they have been doing what God asked all human beings to do! Simply put, serve your fellow man and be kind to each other!

My oldest brother, Henry E. Irby, Jr., has been a serving member of Kappa Alpha Psi Fraternity, Inc. 40 plus years. As a result of his service to so many people in his surrounding communities, he was honored with a scholarship – that is named after him – to assist young Black African Americans males who want to continue their education and learn how to give back and serve others. The Richardson/Plano chapter of Kappa Alpha Psi Fraternity, Inc. awards scholarships each year to young African American males who participate in their Kappa Leadership Development League (Kappa

League), its national mentoring program. One of those scholarships is the Henry E. Irby, Jr. Scholarship award. The phases of Kappa League are as follows:

1. Self-Identity & Purpose: Discipline, Assurance, Awareness, and Appearance

2. Training: Academic, Career Choice, Preparation, Organization

3. Competition: Politics, Career Advancement, and Sports

4. Social: Religion, The Arts, Entertainment, Conversation, Communication, and Etiquette/ Manners

5. Health Education: Physical Fitness-Sex Education-Drugs-Health and Safety

6. Economic Empowerment & Education: Fundamentals of Banking-Earning, Saving, Spending-Saving, Spending-Cash vs. Credit

7. College & Career: Readiness-High School & Beyond

8. Further, this program is for male students in grades 8th-12th

In addition, my other brother, Reverend Kenneth F. Irby, became the pastor of AME Church, St. Petersburg, Florida. Reverend Irby and his First Lady, Karen, planted the seed of an organization, Men in the Making (MIM) and & Women in the Making (WIM) in 1984 in Pontiac, MI. Their original focus of hosting weekend outings started as a simple bait-and-switch for youth. When the teenagers wanted to just play basketball and hang out, they included exposure to teaching life skill strategies in return. Now 40 years later the MIM & WIM curriculum has traveled from Michigan to Long Island, NY, and for the past 10 years it has been in St. Petersburg, FL. MIM & WIM has grown into an amazing role-modeling and mentoring initiative for Black Indigenous People of Color (BIPOC) youth. Women in the Making relaunched eight years ago. Their programs affirm the value of vulnerable children and teaches them how to make the right choices in life as they navigate issues of trauma, peer-pressure, lack of family support and social media. The program provides enrichment, critical thinking and most importantly, positive relationships with caring role models. Accordingly, the data speaks for itself. They are proud to report that 90% of the success of their youth are thriving young adults and affirm the benefits of their wraparound approach. Keeping their youth out of the drop-to-prison pipeline is one of their primary goals. They create intentional pathways to careers and college matriculation. You can learn more by visiting: https://meninthemaking.org/ and https://womeninthemaking.org.

"A new command I give you: Love one another. As I have loved you, so you must love one another. By this everyone will know that you are my disciples, if you love one another." John 13:34- 35 NIV

My Employment

I always had a job from the time I was about 10 years old ironing my Daddy's shirts for $.25 each and doing odd jobs in the neighborhood where I grew up. These odd jobs included washing dishes, running vacuums, hanging clothes on the line, ironing sheets and pillowcases, and of course babysitting infants and toddlers – which was a big deal because that let me know that people trusted me. So, I always had a few dollars in my pocket. But as time went on, life would take me up and down roads and paths that I had never traveled before. Once the disco scene hit the U.S., particularly in the Washington, D.C. area, I found myself dancing and singing in nightclubs part-time, making extra money. Despite the fact I was out on my own, I knew that if my father ever heard about it, he would not appreciate that news falling on his ear drums. At this time in my life, I had real bills to pay, and due to the way I was raised, my bills had to be paid on time. At that time, my rent was $69 a month, all utilities included. Yes. But I had a telephone, and I had recently purchased a brand-new playboy pink with black vinyl roof Mustang that had a car note of $117 per month. There was insurance, food, etc. While my life, at that time, was certainly no tea party, I managed because I had secured employment with Uncle Sam. So, I knew I had real benefits, health insurance coverage, and earning leave to be off from work for sick days, as well as personal days. My first good government job was like what the older people used to say: "If you're lucky enough to get a job in the government, you have hit the jackpot!" Well, I certainly worked long enough in both government and private industry to know that that statement is complete BULL! But while getting out on the world stage of LIFE, you have to start somewhere. I was fortunate enough to jumpstart my career journey as a clerk for the Veterans Administration, central office, in downtown Washington, D.C. – Grade GS-3! You couldn't tell me anything because I knew that I had made it. I had a full-time job, and I was making money at night as a dancer and singer. I was also making money on the weekends serving chicken and chitterling dinners on the side! When the disco scene hit the District of Columbia, my bestie Judy Greenfield and I and a couple of other young girls hit the nightclubs throughout the city: Chez Maurice, Hollywood Club, Wilson Ranch House, Market Inn, cabarets (which you don't hear of anymore). I had to make ends meet because my lifestyle was changing, and I knew that I was on the move to meet my goals, as I had challenged myself to go back to college and finish my degree. In the meantime, I had started another part-time job three days a week at Jennifer Mall, as a janitor supervisor earning $100 per week. I kept that trash tossing and bathroom cleaning YUCK floor buffing gig moving for a year and a half to meet my goal because I only had one year left at Federal City College (FCC) until graduating and securing my degree. It was in September of 1971, when I challenged myself and registered for evening classes at FCC. I was determined to get my degree this time around because I had set that goal before and missed it again. I was determined to accomplish it this time and not screw it up! It was a hot and sticky evening, on a Wednesday, when I entered the building. I was lost and had problems finding my way to my math class. Then I tripped and stumbled over the foot of a tall glass of iced tea – fine as he could be – a gentleman standing outside of a classroom. So, I asked, "Excuse me sir. Do you know where Professor Saunders's classroom is?" He responded, "I'm Professor Saunders, and my classroom is right here." I almost passed out as our eyes locked on each other at the same time, while we were standing in the hallway. Well, the rest is history! Thirty days later on October 26, 1971, Joe Hayes Saunders and I got married at lunch time. I went back to my office, and my then supervisor, Mr. Ireland, said, "You are one hour late from lunch. Please sign a leave slip." When I told him why I was late, he said, "What? Do your parents know that you are getting married today?" I said, "No, they don't because I didn't know that I was getting married either." We didn't have cell phones then! Whew!! Joe called me early that morning and whispered sweet and delicious things in my ear in addition to saying, "Let's get married today." I said, "Why of course," and later on that day, we went across the bridge and got married at lunch time. When I got back into my office, Mr. Ireland said, "Zelda, you just go home and don't come back until Monday because you have caused a ruckus in the office. But this Federal Register still has to get out now this week, but I am sure Sara and Frances will get it done because Ms. Issacson is waiting for the final proofreading to be completed."

Fortunately, prior to starting my good government career, I worked a part-time job after school when I was in the 11th grade at McKinley Tech, as a secretary for Dr. McKinney, on Georgia Avenue, N.W., Washington. So, I had a clue about being responsible on the job.

Chapter 2
I'm a Little Teapot

The innocence of life...

Hurricane Hazel

    I couldn't believe the loud noises that I was hearing coming from the winds of Hurricane Hazel on October 15, 1954. The winds sounded like a freight train, blowing through our community when we lived in the apartments at 315 "G" Street, Northeast, Washington, D.C. I recall that every time Daddy came back inside our apartment, he looked tired and bothered. I heard him tell Mom, "Well, Hazel just snatched another bag right out of my hands." Then I heard Mom say, "I know the winds are blowing real hard, and the sounds are really scary. But I don't care how hard the winds are blowing, or how much rain falls from the sky, we're leaving this apartment today! So please, move those last few bags, get the telephone table on the way out, including the little table and chairs out of the kitchen onto the truck, because we're leaving here today, okay. Honey. Thank you." Most of our other limited belongings were already on the truck. But like a good husband and father, Daddy picked up the items that mom had asked him to get and put them on the truck. We were on our way and moving on up!

New Beginnings

When we finally got moved into our new home at the Woodridge address at 2909 26th Street, Northeast, Washington, D.C., it was dark and raining like crazy. We were tired, hungry, wet, and sleepy, but none of that stopped us from getting our stuff off of the truck and into the house. Mom had an agenda, and we had to meet her standard. We did just that, believing the sun would come out tomorrow, and it did. A few months later, after having moved into our new neighborhood, in which the majority of families were white people, we began to settle in. We got our first puppy, had a fenced in yard, and a garage with a pear tree. Daddy made it clear by telling us, "I believe dogs belong outside." I knew from that moment forward that I would be getting in lots of trouble with him because I already had Humphrey upstairs and in my bed. A couple weeks later, I noticed Humphrey was not looking good. So, I walked him to Rhode Island Avenue to see our community veterinarian, Dr. Webber. His examination results showed that Humphrey had distemper, a canine disease that negatively affects a wide variety of mammals, including dogs, but does not affect human beings. I was brokenhearted to find out there was nothing that could be done to save my pet collie, Humphrey, and I cried all the way back home.

Several weeks passed, and I remembered seeing the older white lady who lived across the street up on the hill. She was so nice, and she loved cats. Our neighbors seemed to distance themselves from her, and she was as white as they were. So, I did just the opposite. I knocked on her door one day, and I couldn't believe my eyes when she opened her door, and I saw all of her cats in her house. By now, I was about eight years old, and we had a great conversation about animals. On that first visit to her house, she offered me one of her black Persian kittens, and I was happy as I could be. I knew that I would have to hide Bubble Stone Brooks (BSB) when I got him inside the house. Mom did not like cats, and my father liked them even less. I took BSB upstairs to my room, put him next to the window well, and he went to sleep. He was black as midnight with beautiful soft hair and gray eyes. He reminded me of a black knight, without the horse of course. Believe it or not, I was able to keep him out of sight for a while until he was ready to eat and started going to the bathroom. That's when I knew the cat was going to be let out of the bag. I begged Mom and Dad to please let me keep him, and they were so kind. I had BSB for a short while. He died so soon after he was gifted to me.

    Shortly thereafter, I was blessed with another cat, a Siamese. SHIM was something else. My mom fell in love with my gorgeous Siamese SHIM. Mom even let SHIM get on her bed with the red comforter covering the bed during Christmas time. SHIM was a chocolate seal point Siamese. She was a gorgeous animal. Unfortunately, several years after becoming the house cat and Mom's favorite animal, I thought I was going to have to give her up.

One day (note, we also had dogs too), Mom had a sinus issue, and she swished salt and water up her nose to get relief. The sounds frightened SHIM, and she attacked mom's lower leg. Well, I just knew that I would have to take SHIM up to Dr. Webber's office to be fostered. Fortunately for SHIM, Mom had a soft spot in her heart for SHIM, and what had happened was an accident. Mom simply said that it was not SHIM's fault. Mom actually told me later that she felt SHIM was protecting her from sounds coming from the bathroom. We took Mom to the hospital, and when we came back from Providence, life went on as usual, and SHIM stayed with us until she crossed the Rainbow Bridge.

School Days

I attended Woodridge Elementary School in September 1954, shortly after Linda Brown versus The Board of Education, when Attorney Thurgood Marshall argued and won the case in front of the Supreme Court of the United States, that negroes could attend schools with whites in certain jurisdictions. Fortunately, for us, the District of Columbia was one of those places, and my brothers and I integrated

Woodridge Elementary School in our community. At the time, our community was majority white, and unfortunately – just about every day – I was in a fight with a white person. Gender didn't matter. Then the conflicts happened right on our block. I remember Susie, who lived two doors up from me, called me a "Nigger" when we were playing with our dolls, not even having a tea party, and I gave her the BLUES afterwards! She never called me that word ever again. When I was in the third grade, one of my buddies, Charlotte, got teased a lot because she had freckles and long thick red hair. We were friends – so I thought – until one day, we were painting and doing a project for school. She turned around and held up a jar of black paint and pointed to the jar, saying, "This is you in a jar." Well, I just happened to have a pair of scissors in my hand, and her plaits fell short. I got expelled from school and punished for a week, but no hands-on! Daddy explained to me that I couldn't retaliate in a negative manner when people called me out of my name. It took me a while to catch up to what he was talking about, and to this day, those experiences hurt me, and I will never forget them. Of course, as time went on, I would come to see the real harm of what racism and discrimination would bring to me up the road in my personal and work experiences.

Being exposed to religion at an early age, I will always remember when we had to go to classes to be confirmed. In the Episcopalian religion, you are confirmed at age 12, and Easter Sunday was the day to have hands laid upon you by our late, beloved Bishop and Father James O. West, Jr. Each and every Sunday, I would go roller skating, from 1:00 until 5:00, on Kalorama Road, Washington, D.C. When I discovered that my confirmation classes would conflict with my joy of skating, I was not happy. So, from October 1959, until the next spring of 1960, I missed skating all of those Sundays, but I was confirmed and blessed by God, through the laying on of hands by our Bishop and Father West. To God be the Glory!

Now, I am attending Taft Jr. High School, and I have to take algebra from a man named Mr. George R. Rhodes. He was a gentle spirit, but I hated math, and he did everything in his power to make me like numbers. Of course, that never happened. But I got through and passed his class knowing in my mind that I would never ever have to see his face again. WOW! Was I WRONG!! Mr. Rhodes would end up being my principal at McKinley Technical High School, and with his higher education experience, Mr. Rhodes became Dr. Rhodes! I couldn't believe my eyes when I saw him in the halls of McKinley, and I asked him, "Sir, what are you doing at McKinley?" He responded, "I'm the principal of McKinley High School." I said, "What happened to Mr. Watts?" Dr. Rhodes said, "He's around." I collected myself and thoughts. I knew this man was kind, but he didn't play. So, I made the necessary adjustments because he would be my principal for the next four years, and believe it or not, we simply became best friends like so many of his students. I formally eulogized him at his funeral. Dr. Rhodes, along with some of our favorite teachers, attended our 20th and 30th year high school reunions.

At our 20th year class reunion, Dr. Rhodes anointed us with his favorite song. We were his second class graduating from the great halls of McKinley Tech. The song, "Ain't No Stopping Us Now" was recorded by artists, McFadden & Whitehead in 1979. My class of 1966, was the class that rebelled against the system because the leadership didn't want us to do anything except learn, eat lunch, do our homework and go home. Of course, we wanted to learn and get our schoolwork done, but we wanted to participate in other activities as well, so we were the CLASS of 1966 that PROTESTED everything! For example, we wanted to have real homecoming activities, not only for the football game, but we wanted a HOMECOMING DANCE, a queen court, and all of the festivities that resembled an actual homecoming gala! AND WE DID!! When we were in high school, we could take drivers education. Upon my sweet 16, Valentine's Day birthday, I got my learner's permit, and I was a happy camper.

Growing Up with Brothers

After my oldest brother graduated from McKinley in 1963, and I had passed my driving test, it was now my turn to drive my Daddy's two-toned turquoise and beige '56 Chevy up onto the great parking lot of McKinley Tech Plaza and park the car. In the midst of me preparing to go downtown to the Department of Motor Vehicle to get my learner's permit on my sweet 16, Valentine's Day birthday, I changed my dress and put it on Kenny Boy's bed. As I was going down the steps, he was coming up and went into his room. He started to yell and later picked up my dress and threw it on the floor. I said, "Come on

Kenny Boy, I'm in a hurry." He said, "Girl, you better take that dress off my bed." I responded, "I just told you that I'm in a hurry because I have to get downtown to take my driving test to get my learner's permit today because I am a sweet 16 years of age." He would not let it go. In the meantime, I changed my mind and changed into another red dress. This time, Kenny Boy threw that dress on the floor as well. Now it was on between us. We were exchanging words that were not *kool* and moved ourselves and words into the hallway right by the top of steps. Our exchange of words was hot, and before I knew it, he had blocked my way to keep me from going down the steps. So, I politely flipped him over my shoulder and watched him fall gracefully down the stairs into the view of our father. Fortunately, for me, our father had not left for work yet and happened to be standing at the bottom of the steps. He saw how I had flipped Kenny Boy over my shoulder, and he saw Kenny Boy coming down the steps.

Daddy looked up at him and said, "Kenny Boy, I told you and your brother to leave Sassy alone, and that one day she would retaliate. Today's her lucky day, and you had better not touch her." I have so many sweet memories of how I survived being raised with my two brothers. At the beginning or the end of any day, I love my brothers, and they love their only sister on earth!

Sweet Memories

We were fortunate to have family to babysit us from time to time. My darling cousin, Jean Robinson White, the Original Babysitter (OBS), took care of me and my brothers during the time we lived at 315 "G" Street, N.E., Apt. #202, Washington, D.C., until she went to college. Then Aunt Frankie came to live with us while we lived in the apartment. So, she took care of us for a spell, as well as Mrs. Louise Lockhart, who lived across the street from our apartment building. Mrs. Lockhart used to look in on us as well, and then, on October 15, 1954, the same day Hurricane Hazel smashed into D.C., we moved to 2909 26th Street, N.E., Washington, D. C. My mother, Mrs. Elizabeth Josephine Powell Irby, said, "We are leaving this apartment today. I don't care what's happening outside. We are leaving. Come Henry and call us each by name. Let's go." I remember it as if it were yesterday. We left 315 "G" Street with rain, wind, and crap blowing out of our hands and up into the air like kites. Today, Jeannie, who will be 90 years old March 12, 2024, Lord willing, tells me that when I was a baby, I smiled most of the time and that I was a good and happy baby. My best guess is that Jeannie started calling me Sassy Mae because she picked it up from hearing my father call me that nickname. Jean and my father had something in common, as they always talked about the power of voting and service to others. My darling cousin, Jeannie, still calls me Sassy Mae to this day. As a matter of fact, my first experience voting for the President of the United States of America was one of the highlights of my life at that time. I still remember me and Daddy going around to vote together in the 1968 Presidential election at Woodridge Elementary where I went to grade school. I really wanted to vote for Lyndon B. Johnson (LBJ), but I was one year shy of my eighteenth birthday and had to wait for the next cycle in which Richard M. Nixon ran for the top office in the free world. He won the presidency, only to have to leave it in disgrace for the obstruction of justice and other crimes he had committed against American citizens to stay in power. But Barry Goldwater was not having it, and Nixon did his salute and flew away like a bat despite it being daylight. Who knew that fifty years later the American citizens would see a repeat of this poor and sick behavior in our lifetime from another sitting President! But I was so proud and happy as my father taught me and my brothers about the power of voting, the importance of serving people in your communities, and being kind to people.

Of course, being the God-fearing man that he was, attending church every Sunday was a major part of my upbringing. Sometimes, we got it right, and sometimes we missed our mark. When we missed our mark, we were reminded and punished for our misdeeds by having phone and car privileges taken away. Of course, later on in my life, I never dreamed that I would ever see a Black man become President of the free world. I was thrilled the night when I was watching CNN, and anchor, Wolf Blitzer called Barack Hussein Obama's name as victorious in the state of Virginia and that Obama would become the first Black man to win the presidency. The WORLD went crazy happy for a spell, but members of the Tea Party and other white nationalist groups lost their minds. The "Obama Bashing" took on a life of its own. It continues to have energy today, as the former 45th President of the United States of America, is now identified as a convicted criminal on 34 counts and is awaiting sentencing, which is scheduled for July 11, 2024. I am not holding my breath for him to serve any jail time, as any other criminal would already be behind bars awaiting to be sentenced. As I reflect on the attacks on our Capitol on January 6, 2021, the outcomes appear to be ongoing as citizens are still suffering, while others rejoice. Our freedoms and liberties for justice are diminishing and our rights keep getting overturned – ROE v. WADE for starters. There's no question in my mind that DEMOCRACY, as I have known it, is slipping away. I just pray the masses get out and VOTE in November 2024. Otherwise, as Whoopi Goldberg stated in the movie *Ghost*, "Molly, girl, you're in danger" – or something similar. Also, when I reflect on some of the stories that my parents shared, it's not shocking to me that history is repeating itself because the mentality of the so-called leadership of both houses of Congress is the same. NONE of the laws have been legislated to eliminate bad and sick behavior of citizens who continue to practice racism activities in the workplace, surrounding communities, and now, right up close and personal in both houses of Congress. I have been alive long enough to know that our Congress behaves in the manner in which they do because there are some Americans who vote and allow them to be seated in the people's house. Until the majority of people register to vote these clowns out of office, NOTHING is going to get done, and not much shall change. Fortunately, I am blessed to participate and vote in the upcoming Presidential election, God willing, and I believe He'll let me participate. With a population of increasing numbers of people of color, I do not believe there is any reason to fool yourself or to be fooled by others. Simply put, with all of the misinformation and social media platforms, the state of confusion is exactly where the politicians want voters to be so that they can obtain more control over the masses. It breaks my heart – not my spirit – to see so many people being led around by the tip of their nose, not doing their research, and just accepting conspiracies from charlatans trying to deceive and push false claims to win elections. This is happening at all levels – from local elections up to the federal level, all the way to the Supreme Court. But our parents played it as safe as they could with us by sharing current information from the local newspaper, (i.e., *Daily News*, the *Washington Post*, and *The Times*). All three papers were always under our roof because our father read the newspapers every day and would inform us about what was happening until we became old enough to read and come to our own safe conclusions on how to move out of the house.

When school would close for the summer or holidays, I would be dropped off at 412 "H" Street, N.E., at my Aunt Janice's and Uncle Palmer's to spend most of summer down in the country. Kenny Boy would be taken over to Aunt Norma's in Barry Farm, and Henry Jr., (aka Dickie), would go to Kemper Road, in Arlington, VA. Daddy, oftentimes, would be concerned because he wanted us to spend some summers with his brothers and sisters, in Greenville, South Carolina, but Mom said that none of her children would be allowed to go any further south than the state of Virginia. We did not go any further south until we were grown and made the decision on our own to do so. I was happy to meet my cousins because by now as a grown individual, most of my dad's siblings had passed from this world. But his oldest sister, my Aunt Bert, a double amputee due to diabetes, would come up from Greenville, South Carolina, to visit her baby brother, and we would have a great time together. When our family members from Baltimore knew that Aunt Bert and her sons were coming to visit Daddy, they would come over to our house on 26th Street, we would have a cookout in the backyard, we would have a ball. Most of the time when Aunt Bert came up to visit, it was around her birthday, ending in June. Now this topic comes up every two years when the reunions are held, and there will always be a dispute about how the reunion got started. But I know how the IRBY-JONES reunion got started because it started in my backyard when Aunt Bert came to visit her baby brother, my father. This tea will get spilled repeatedly now and until the end of time. I am convinced that's really when and how the IRBY-JONES Family Reunions started. I was thrilled that Aunt Bert lived long enough to meet and hold my daughter before she transitioned to heaven. Aunt Bert had fourteen, so I had lots of cousins to meet as we gathered for upcoming family reunions.

Chapter 3
Reading the Tea Leaves

What does the future hold for me....

Graduation

    Shortly before leaving the McKinley Tech Plaza for the final time as a student, I went down the hallway to go to my locker and change my shoes and slip on my gray hush puppies. My play sister, Casey, was standing in front of my locker with the door opened. Back in the time of my high school days, best friends used to sometimes share lockers, or we would know each other's locker combination numbers. Casey was standing there with my gray hush puppies in her hand. I said, "Why do you have my shoes?" She responded, "Zelda, it's time to throw these runover puppies in the trash." I said, "Casey, those are the most comfortable pair of shoes that I own." We laughed and started walking down the hallway to the gym to say goodbye to Mrs. Stone and our other teachers. When we passed the big trash can, Casey tossed my puppies into the can. She kept walking towards the gym, and I caught up to her after I pulled my puppies out of the trash because those were my favorite puppies, and I was not ready to throw them away! It was getting late into the day. We had to get home and go to work because we had jobs. We had started working even before we graduated. Our class of 1966 was actually the last group of students who graduated from the McKinley High School auditorium.

Life After High School

Several weeks later, I had left the nest from around the corner on 26th Street and moved around the other corner to my extended Herbert family on Girard Place. The efficiency apartment, now called studios, that I had applied for was located at 1618 3rd floor Irving Street, N.E., Washington, D.C. However, my apartment would not be ready for occupancy for a couple of months. The efficiency apartment rentals were limited at that building, and $69 a month – including all utilities – was all that I could afford at that time in my life. Ma and Pap Herbert were so kind and loving enough, including their eight children, to let me and Casey share the basement, and we had a ball. Both of us were working, paying rent, and buying our food (including those Murray Steaks that were so delicious back in the day). The only difference was that I had two jobs because I was preparing to be on my own out there in the world for real, and I needed extra money for the installation of my then C&P cord dial telephone, orange shag rug, almond green futon couch, car note, insurance, etc. Whew!! During this time in our young lives and despite the differences in size – I was short, and Casey was tall – we found ourselves dressing like twins in a lot of situations. I remember the time we went on one of the Annual Sportsman's Boat rides down the Potomac River. On this particular ride down the river, we were dressed alike and looked pretty good in our navy, red, white polka dots, and yellow ruffle outfits and red sandals! We had so much fun on that boat ride. Unfortunately, on the way back from Marshall Hall, a fight broke out on the boat. A few folks had actually jumped overboard to avoid being hit and or knocked out because fists were flying, along with bottles, food, shoes, etc. Casey and I had to come up with a plan that once the boat docked, we would take off and run like the wind to get to a safe spot until we could get back home. I actually ran so fast that I ran out of one of my sandals. I simply lost it, and when we got back downtown, I had one sandal. Casey said, "Zelda, where is your other sandal?" I responded, "I ran out of it. It's gone." We got a cab and got back home and talked about that adventure for a long time. As a matter of fact, we just laughed about it not too long ago. Although we had boyfriends, we would go out on the town and attend community activities and events without them because a lot of times they didn't want to go with us. So, we would go out and do our own thing and would see them later. At the time, I was dating P.L. Williams, who attended and graduated from Easter High School, but he was getting ready to go to Vietnam. He asked me to marry him. Of course, I said, "No." I knew that I was too young to be getting married. Furthermore, I had a plan to attend college and get my own apartment and make some money since my singing career had failed miserably. In the meantime, Casey was dating too, and she had a plan to go out West. One evening we got into some trouble with Pap Herbert, and he told us we could not have any company for the evening because we had missed our curfew. Of course, it was late. Casey and I decided to wait until Pap Herbert went up and went to bed, and we would go ahead with our plan. Simply put, when we thought the coast was clear, we opened the back door to the basement and let our boyfriends inside. We wanted to talk some more, hug, and kiss them like normal. No. We were not stupid girls to do anything like have sex under Ma & Pa Herbert's roof and then be put out of the house for good without a place to live!! Soon after P.L. and Robin were inside, we sat down on the sofa bed in our room, turned the radio on and had it real low, and we started to dance. All of a sudden, P.L. said, "I hear someone coming down the stairs." Casey told Robin to get under the bed, P.L. got under the covers, and I sat on top of him. When Pap Herbert looked over and said, "Who is down here with y'all?" Of course, we said in harmony, "Ain't nobody down here but us Daddy." When Pa Herbert went back up the stairs, P.L. and Robin got out that basement back door so fast they looked like a lightning rod had just landed. The next morning, we went upstairs for breakfast, and Pa Herbert told us that he had seen P.L. and Robin through the backyard to get out front to their cars. Casey and I just looked at each other and didn't say a word! As time moved forward, Casey finally decided to leave the area, marry and go out West. Our lives would keep changing, but we always stayed in touch with each other despite our various challenges in life with children, family, and husbands. Our sistahood and girl friendship keeps us close until the day God calls us to be at home, back up in the universe to be with Him where we started out. Cassandra Antoinette Herbert Gross McMorris, I love you, my sister, forever.

My Friend, Zenobia

It was so cold outside this particular day, but I had to go visit one of my dear friends in Southwest Washington, D.C. I got off the bus and walked up the street to my friend's house, rang the doorbell, and her mom opened the front door and greeted me saying, "Well it's been a long time since I saw your face. How are you doing other little daughter?" I replied, "Hi Mom-E. I'm doing just fine. Where's my sister?" "She's downstairs in the basement doing laundry and playing those "45s" y'all like so much. I just heard the song, "You Really Got

A Hold On Me" by the Miracles. Go on down there." I started down the steps, calling out her name. She didn't respond, so I called out to her again. Still no answer. So, I said, "Okay it's just me – your girl Zelda. Come on out wherever you are because I didn't catch the crosstown bus all of the way from Northeast to Southwest to play hide and seek. Plus, we are too old for that game anymore anyway. Where are you, Zenobia?!" And there she was sitting over in the corner with a cloudy plastic bag over her head. I rushed over, snatched the bag off from her head and asked, "What the hell is wrong with you?" She responded, "Be quiet and don't tell Momma. She would be sick if she knew what I was doing. I said, "Hell, I am sick of what you're trying to do." I demanded her to tell me what was happening, otherwise, I was telling Mom-E right away. Zenobia grabbed my hand and begged me not to be so loud, and then she said in a soft voice, "Girl, I am pregnant!!!" I almost passed out. I said "WHAT?! How did that happen?" She said, "Do not be stupid. You know how it happened." Then I started to call out names of her boyfriends. She said, "None of them. I was raped and didn't tell anybody because I felt that no one would believe me." After I caught my breath, I sat down on the floor beside her and began to think about what and how to help my best friend to resolve her dilemma. Just as we were getting up off the floor, Mom-E had come down the steps to bring us some chips and soda and started talking about stuff that we were not interested in but had to listen to her rant. She was sick of her supervisor at work, and she couldn't wait to retire in about 20 more years from then. After Mom-E had left the room and gone back upstairs, Zoe and I began talking about a strategy for how to resolve her particular matter of being raped and now pregnant. We simply cried, talked, hugged, and cried some more because for the first time in our still young teenage lives, we were actually experiencing a real-life crisis situation. We had no clue about where to turn or who to talk with about both matters. As the oldest one between us, I decided to talk with one of my favorite adult friends who was like a play aunt. I knew she would know how to help us handle the situation involving Zenobia.

    A couple weeks later, Zoe came over to visit me and we went to visit my play aunt to discuss the topics of rape and pregnancy. When we arrived at my aunt's beautiful apartment, we were surprised by the really nice meal she had fixed for us. Later, she showed us how to play a card game called canasta. Upon completing our lessons on learning how to play canasta – since my aunt had a clue about why we were there in the first place – she started asking the real hard questions. She was not for any foolishness either. Out of the gate, Zoe started crying, and my aunt was extremely sympathetic to why Zoe was waterfalling. Then all of a sudden, I opened my mouth to make a contribution to the conversation, and my aunt politely shut me down. We finally left her beautiful apartment with a plan of knowing that Zoe would be alright in the upcoming months. However, from the conversation with my aunt, both the police would be notified, along with Zoe's parents. They need to know what was coming down the pike because it involved their only child's health, credibility, and the future of her reputation. I was happy when Zoe's situation became resolved, and she will always have a space in my heart and mind because our spirits are identical.

Sista Girl Friendship

Growing up it was not always easy developing friendships. Fortunately, from the time I was a little girl in grade school, I was blessed then and to this day with my friends: Cassandra A. Herbert McMorris, Betty B. Butler, Fannie Jo Wynn Tate, (RIP) Patricia Bandy Robinson, and Sandra Holland Handon. I grew up with them, and today, they remain my sista girlfriends. I consider our "SISTA GIRL FRIENDSHIP" an extension of family. It's a blessing because so many people get caught up in situations that oftentimes never get resolved. Some folks leave the land of the living not speaking or talking to each other for reasons they may have been able to resolve had they just reached out and believed through the grace and love of God. Forgiveness is key in all relationships because none of us are perfect despite living the best life we know how to on God's planet earth. A long time ago, while growing up, I believed that I had a best friend who taught me the true definition of what a charlatan is. From that very painful and blinded experience, I learned some lessons, while walking through those episodes of my life. I learned that God provides us with tools like the element of time and forgiveness to be healed and move on from any bad environmental situations involving any human being or particular things. I have come to know and understand that as human beings we are supposed to use each other – NOT MISUSE each other! There is a difference between the two traits. Only we have the power to examine and know how to differentiate between those traits whenever they show up in our path or relationships – personally or in the workforce.

Class of 1966

Reflecting on when I was in high school at McKinley Tech: Fortunately, my class was the second group of ninth graders who attended Tech. So, I graduated from McKinley Tech twice – once from the ninth grade, and again in 1966 from the 12th grade. Our class of 1966 was truly historic because we were the last class that graduated from the auditorium, and the first class to actually conduct homecoming activities. We had a football game, an entire talent show for the student body to choose their first Queen and her court, and a full formal dance. Our school student body was ready to make changes in the world, but we had to make some within our own learning environment too. We were a smart, political group of kids. I remember the BIG NEWS back in the day was about the Mississippi Bus Boycott that started in December 1955, as the

Reverend Dr. Martin Luther King, Jr. had become the leader of American negroes. We had an Upper House and Lower House at McKinley, and I was a member of the Lower House. I ran track, played volleyball, and made some of my clothes through the teaching of one of my neighbors, including my Home Economics teacher, Miss Beck! I even tried out for the cheerleaders' squad, but I missed it by one point off on my report card. I was First Runner-Up for Homecoming Queen, and my sista girlfriend Fannie Jo Wynn Tate (RIP), was in the Queen's Court too. My class of 1966 was the first class at Tech who bucked the system about everything because we wanted some of the rules and standards to change. Trust and believe things changed BIG TIME! Yes! We got in trouble, but it was good! There are so many wonderful things to say about the McKinley Way, but I may have to save that topic of discussion for simply another tea party.

Dorells

Back in the day, I used to love to sing in the morning, noon, and nighttime. My parents were excellent singers too. My daddy was a heck of a tenor singer, as he carried notes and tones Eddie Kendricks of the Temptations would have envied. Every Sunday morning, Daddy woke us up singing "Precious Lord" or "Eye on the Sparrow" – still two of my favorite spirituals. My mother had a beautiful soprano voice, and I found myself copying her, but the tone of my voice was more contralto. When I was much younger, I could complete falsetto, and I performed falsetto on my first recording, "Maybe Baby," as well as on our second recording, flip side, "You Are." So many artists who recorded found themselves doing falsettos in the event they had a cold or simply couldn't hit that note at that particular time and couldn't fool their audience in real time at a live performance. My brothers and I used to sing around the house when songs came on the radio and when our family got together at 3517 South Kemper Road – when Uncle Doug would come to visit from New Jersey. He would get on the piano, and we would start singing anything that came to mind. During the summer months before being shipped off to our summer destinations – Dickie to Kemp Road, me to Aunt Janice's and Uncle Palmer's, and Kenny Boy to Aunt Norma's – we would sometimes participate and sing with other kids under the lamp posts or just listen to them sing. Some of the groups, whether popular or not, had fabulous voices and could sing. Fortunately, enough, I was one of those kids who could sing and was not shy about singing in front of people. Whenever opportunities became available for me to participate in a community talent show, I was there with bells on singing to the top of my lungs because I enjoyed singing. To this day, I recall that when I was eight years old, I participated in my first talent show in elementary school. I performed the song, "Why Do Fools Fall In Love" by Frankie Lymon and The Teenagers, and I won first prize, which was an announcement that "Zelda won the talent show!" From that day forward, I knew that I wanted to sing in another talent show and win, but for whatever reason, I didn't want to sing alone. I believe that I wanted to sing in a group because group singing was so popular, and it was kool to be lead singer. So, in my next singing adventure, I participated in another talent show and won again. This time around, I sang the hit song, "In the Still of the Night," by the Five Satins and won! By now, I was at Taft Jr. High school. There were several boy and girl singing groups all over the place – from northeast, northwest, southeast, and the southwest of Washington, D.C. With plenty of talent show opportunities in our surrounding communities to participate in, I wanted to be in all of them. The very first group that I formed was more like a choir because there were so many of us. It was called The Royal Corvettes. Later, for three of us, we would become the Dorells. We had stiff competition from other girl groups, but we kept on signing and winning talent shows until we became professional recording artists. Our talent show participation had come to an end with great sadness for me because I used to love singing for people in our neighborhoods. IT WAS PURE JOY AND FUN! Now it was just me, Beverly (Amshatar), and Renee' because Janice Rodgers left the group along with a couple of others. Now, as freshmen at McKinley High School, we were the Dorells, and we were gearing up to record our first hit record, "Maybe Baby" – flipped side "The Beating of My Heart," which would later land on local radio station charts at number one for three weeks in a row. One of the original group members was Janice Rodgers. I tried everything to find her, but she left the community. Janice was so sweet, kind, gifted, and talented. She wrote a song entitled "Young Fool" just for me to sing in the first McKinley Tech talent show competition for Homecoming Queen. I won first runner-up in the first McKinley High School homecoming queen court activity in the history of the school! The student body elected their queen of the first homecoming. I was first runner-up, and the other members of the court included Fannie Jo Wynn, Joan Christopher, and Jamesina Burns. My brother, Dickie, was a senior at Tech. I had the opportunity to drive up onto the parking lot of McKinley Plaza, park my father's 1956 Chevy, meet up with my girls, and sing before the school bell rang for all of us to get to our homerooms and start another day of educational experience and fun life at Tech – where singing was always on the agenda. Now in 1963, if you had decent grades, you might be invited to dance on Teenarama, a dance party show at WOOK radio station. On occasion, I had the privilege to dance on the Teenarama dance party show, and it was BIG FUN. Plus, if you were lucky, you would get a chance to be in a Miles'-long sandwich commercial (invitation only by Mr. Bob King) and eat the sandwich and share it with friends. I got that opportunity once and never dreamed that I would ever be asked to record a record! Get ready because here comes the ASK!

We were coming out of the ladies' room downstairs at the daily

Teenarama dance party show, which aired in Washington, D.C., on WOOK-TV from 1963 until 1970. Like always, me, Beverly (Amshatar), and Renee' were always singing somewhere. All we ever needed was room and space, we would light a joint up and sing because we enjoyed singing together and our harmony was tight as a drum! On this particular day, a guy named K. Washington approached us after he heard us singing and said, "Hey, Zelda. Y'all sound good." I replied, "Yes! We do, thanks." He said would you like to record a record, and of course, we looked at each other like this dude had just lost his mind. We started laughing and walking away like young teenage girls and went up to dance with our classmates during the Teenarama dance party hours. We didn't have that long to dance, and I loved to dance as well as sing. On this particular show, Mr. Bob King invited me to participate in the Miles'-long sub sandwich commercial we used to do on the show. I got to eat that sandwich, and of course I shared it with my friends. Later, I saw K. Washington again. He was walking towards me with a piece of paper in his hand with a telephone number. He asked me to call him if I want my group to record a record. In exchange, I gave K. Washington my telephone number. Shortly thereafter, we had a conversation about the details. Before we knew it, we had a group meeting with our parents because they had to sign our contracts before we could go into the studio, as we were 14- and 15-year-old teenagers.

As young girls, we were blessed to have been raised in two-parent family environments. We were doubly blessed with two brothers in each one of our families. Beverly's (Amshatar) parents (RIP) were Mr. Melvin and Mrs. Dorothy Monroe, and her brothers were, Reggie (RIP) and Ronald (RIP). Renee's parents (RIP) were Mr. Joseph and Mrs. Pollyanna Morris, and her brothers were Joe (RIP) and Wayne (RIP). My parents (RIP) were Mr. Henry E. Irby, Sr. and Mrs. Elizabeth Irby. I am blessed with my brothers Henry Jr. (aka "Dickie") and Kenneth ("Kenny Boy") – Reverend K.F. Irby.

I remember like it was yesterday. The weather was cold and dreary. It was really early on a Saturday when we met down on "K" Street, N.W., Washington, D.C. and walked into the recording studio. The Rick Henderson Band was firing up their instruments and getting in place as our musicians, as we were gearing up to engage in our first ever exciting recording experience as the group known as the Dorells! I just remember feeling like crap that Saturday morning when I woke up because I was recovering from a sore throat and head cold the previous week. But I knew within my heart, mind, and spirit that I was not going to miss out on this experience to record a song with Beverly (Amshatar) and Renee' because I had always dreamed of recording a record. So, dreams do come true, and now you are reading my book. Yes! Dreams do come true! PRAISE THE LORD! All you have to do is believe and have a plan of action to bring life to your dreams. Whether they are successful or not is another book completely. I was so nervous when we got downtown to the studio on "K" Street, N.W. – despite feeling like crap and excited all at the same time. Once we got inside of the studio room, I became excited and could not talk for a minute. I thought to myself, *"What in the heck is going on with me?"* I knew it was nerves, and I got myself together after I started hearing instruments and the guys talking about the lyrics they wanted us to sing. One of the exciting elements about the entire experience was that we had never met the people who were in charge and wanted us to record. They came over, introduced themselves, and told us who the manager was and who wrote the songs. By now, I had started to cough, and a couple of times they wanted to know if I was alright. I told them that I was recovering from a head cold and sore throat, but I was feeling better. They offered me a cup of hot tea with lemon and sugar. I drank it, and I was alright. Apparently, I was better because for the first time, I read the words to the song "Maybe Baby" and "The Beating of My Heart" and sang my vocal folds to the max. I do remember us having to record several times. On the last try of recording the original pressing of the record, one of the owners, Eugene Todd, asked me to step into a booth by myself. Beverly (Amshatar) and Renee' stepped into the other booth, and my best guess is that they later blended our voices on the recording. After about five recordings, we, The Dorells, had recorded our first record entitled, "Maybe Baby" with "The Beating of my Heart" on the flip side. We were on a roll and as happy as could be. The original song was recorded on the G.E.L. label, and later, we crossed over and recorded on Atlantic Records. We were so young, fourteen and fifteen years old, in 1962 and 1963. "Maybe Baby" was released in 1964. I remember it was during Easter weekend, and my mom had picked me up from choir rehearsal from Calvary. On our way back home, WOOK-100 was on the air, and all of a sudden, I heard the strings of that guitar from one of the players in Rick Henderson's band. I screamed out loud and said to my mother, "Mom, stop the car. Stop the car. That's us singing on the radio." My mother said, "Girl. What are you talking about?" I went on telling her that our record was being played on the radio, but she kept on driving and didn't miss one turn. Of course, by the time she knew what I was talking about, the record had gone off and another record was being played. When we got into the house, I told Kenny Boy and Daddy what was happening. Neither one of them was ever as excited as I was. My other brother, Dickie, had already left the house and neighborhood for college, but at a later time, he got to hear my group singing one day with some of his college roommates. My joy and level of enthusiasm to become teenage recording artists was over the moon. I imagined Beverly (Amshatar) and Renee' felt the same excitement that The Supremes, The Shirelles, Martha & Vandellas, and other Motown Hitsville USA and famous Doo-Wop group singers shared when they recorded their first record for the world to hear! As time went on, we were still in high school but no longer allowed to participate in school talent show activities around town because we were professional recording artists. Being restricted from being in upcoming talent shows in surrounding local communities made me sad because we enjoyed singing and participating in community talent shows back in my day. It was BIG FUN! But it felt good walking the halls of McKinley High School with our student body recognizing us as professional recording artists. To this day, when I see some of my classmates from Taft Jr. High or McKinley, some still ask me if I sing. Of course, my answer to them is that I don't sing anymore since I stopped smoking 14 years ago.

My vocal folds changed tremendously, and I can't sing anymore. I am not one who you will ever see trying to hit a note knowing that I can't carry that tune. Honestly, it breaks my heart when I see and hear singing artists who have passed their prime time, yet they are still trying to hit notes they already know they can't carry anymore. It's embarrassing and hurts my feelings, and I feel bad for them and their sweet memories of the good old days that have passed.

One of my reflections is when I visited a record store that was going out of business. I happened to see a CD entitled *Shake Rattle Rarest of the Rare, Volume 8*. When I turned the CD box over, I discovered that my second recording, "Good Luck to The Lucky Girl," recorded on RSVP label in 1965 and dubbed number three, was on this particular CD. So many singing groups from back in the day, during the Doo-Wop era – and even before – never got paid any money for their talent. My group never received one thin DIME or royalties either. DISGUSTING! WE NEVER GOT PAID! HOW ABOUT A THIN DIME?! NOPE! As time went by and I aged a bit, I ventured out and paid money to various lawyers trying to find out how to get paid. After a period of time had passed, I realized that I had wasted more money seeking a way to obtain what I believed we should have been paid, I gave up the struggle and moved on. I chalked it up to another life experience that had failed. I surely had a great time and hold onto the sweet memories of the songs and recordings. They both will be in place forever with my name, Beverly's (Amshatar), and Renee's attached as the Dorells! That's how life "R". I will forever be grateful to my classmate and brother, Warren "Scooter" Magruder, for his ongoing support of The Dorells from the time we became recording artists back in high school. I am convinced that "Maybe Baby" could be one of Scooter's favorites records or songs because he still plays it on the radio today. People who listen to his show can hear our record. Thank you, Scooter, for your love, time, and attention to us over the many years – despite us never getting paid for recording "Maybe Baby" and "Good Luck to the Lucky Girl." By the way, should you ever come across a copy of either record again, please let me know because I would like to buy an un-played copy of each to leave behind for my grandson, Enzo, in memory of his Grand-Zee!

In the spring of 2023, as original creator and lead singer of my group, The Dorells, I was invited by Beverly Lindsay-Johnson to an event. Lindsay-Johnson is an Emmy award winning television producer, entertainment consultant, public relations consultant, and member of the Board of the Atlanta Doo-Wop Association. Beverly continues to work tirelessly to keep Doo-Wop and hand dancing alive in the minds and on the hearts of citizens in the District of Columbia, including people around the globe who still enjoy the Doo-Wop sound. I was tickled when she asked me to participate and to be honored in an open forum discussion of song and group, *A Musical Journey, in the celebration of DC-Doo-Wop, From The*

Street Corner To The Stage. The event was Sunday, July 9, 2023. Pictures of my group, "The Dorells" were displayed on the wall of fame at the Reverend Dr. Martin Luther King, Jr. Library, Washington, District of Columbia. Since the activity was free and open to the general public, people showed up and had a great time with us. One of the many highlights of the event was when I asked my grandson Enzo to bring me the bag that had my original records that the other records had been pressed from. When Enzo came up to me on the stage, folks gave him a grand old clap, and his smile could have melted snow. He kissed me on the cheek and said, "Grand- Zee, I am having fun, but I am going back to my seat to seeing my cousins and mommy." A couple more high points during the discussion was with S. Hylton, MC., one of my old boyfriends that I had not seen in over 50 plus years. He introduced me to the audience, and the curator began his interview with me. Brother Hylton and I liked each other back in the day, but we were simply meant to be friends. I introduced him to one of my girlfriends, and today, they remain friends and have a lovely daughter who is one of my extended nieces. But when Hylton and I saw each other, we hugged and blessed each other's souls for wellbeing. Mark Puryear, the curator, started his interview process with the lead singer and original member of the Rainbows. Mr. Ronald "Poozie" Miles (RIP) was 87 years old. He looked good and sounded great as he performed one of his group's hit records, "Mary Lee" (1950s). Unfortunately, Mr. Miles, passed from this life, six months after the Doo-Wop event, on January 23, 2024. It was such a joy to have shared in his space at the MLK, Jr. Library in the celebration of music and song elements of life that he enjoyed. Mark continued his interview with Mr. Sidney Barnes of The Embracers/Rotary Connection. It was a joy being on stage with Mr. Barnes, as well, as he continues writing and creating music for individuals who dream big and seek to explore many elements of the musical industry. Then the curator sought my attention and began asking me questions about my career as a singer and how we got started singing as a group. Believe it or not, I spilled some tea on him. Simply put, I ended up flipping the script on the curator, and I started asking him questions. I asked his last name, his age, and where he grew up – all places not four blocks from where I grew up. Specifically, his last name had been carved into my brain from many days gone by. Meaning, after all of the questions Mark had answered yes to, I had determined that his late mother had been my 4th grade teacher at Woodbridge Elementary, and that he was in the oven when she was my teacher. That was a spilled tea moment that I could not let go by, and I shared that one with the entire audience at the MLK Library event. Mark laughed out loud so hard it led me to believe that he enjoyed the journey that I took him on when I told him about my findings, and they were true. That is why I knew he was my teacher's son – the last of nine born in his family – and that he lived on Myrtle Avenue, Washington, D.C.

While my group never made it big in the arena of singing artists, I remember that for the short time we were together, we had lots of fun. I still hold a special place in my heart for my dear friend, Janice Rodgers, who wrote a song just for me entitled "Young Fool." I performed her original and beautiful song during the talent show as a participant in the first ever McKinley High School homecoming queen court activity, class of 1966! I didn't win the title, "Queen." However, while I don't know where Janice is today, I pray that she is healthy, happy, and enjoying her best life. Also, my prayers are for Beverly (Amshatar), Renee', and for all of the girls who sang with me back in the day when we sang in talent shows. May all of the girls who I met along the way remain safe, healthy, and happy in whatever endeavors they have chosen, as life took each one of us in different directions as we grew and became independent women. Over time, I have thought about and will forever miss one of the nicest human beings that I have ever met on the face of the earth – my friend – Jossalyn Gill. She was a smart, kind, compassionate, and extremely talented designer. She would sew together any pieces of materials you had in hand and make you one fabulous and original outfit for all time. Jossalyn made several outfits for me for special occasions for our McKinley reunion activities, including my 40th P.J. Valentine's Day birthday celebration because I wanted something unique and a Jossalyn original design. I cannot sport any of the outfits anymore because I have outgrown them. Maybe one of these days, I'll meet an individual who will be able to fit the original outfits designed by Jossalyn, so they too, can appreciate and have another exciting day in their life to look good and be noticed by anyone who is not blind. May Jossalyn's soul forever rest in paradise and be at peace because she was a wonderful individual who carried a sweet and generous spirit while she lived.

As our choices in life would take us in different directions, I had a successful career in the federal government. I also volunteered for various community service programs. I volunteered for hospice, fundraised for CFC, served as a 50+ volunteer, served on the Adult Public Guardianship Review Board. I raised my lovely, smart, and talented daughter, Allison. I am blessed that years later, she delivered a healthy, happy, male to the planet – my loving grandson, Enzo. God blessed me to work, live long enough, stay healthy to retire and to enjoy the rest of my journey here on earth, mark off items from my bucket list, and travel to special places and attend unique events. To God be the Glory!

Chapter 4
Steeped Tea Stirs the Soul

Where my flavor and nutrients were born...

Camper Experience

Several years after my grandmother passed from this world on June 9, 1975, a few of my aunts and uncles had a great idea. They decided to use the land down in the country, as we used to say, for recreation. This great suggestion awakened our huge family into becoming campers from all generations, and we had a BLAST from about 1977 until late 1989 or early 1990s. Early on, at the beginning of our new adventure as new and exciting campers, my Great Uncle really enjoyed us visiting him. However, we came to learn soon enough, that he was not so pleased about seeing all of us so frequently.

Once again, the element of time fixed that situation, and Great Uncle came around to us being on the land as often as we wanted (i.e. every holiday, which meant at least 12 times a year or whenever we, the FAMILY, decided to have a reunion or a special cookout event). During the mid 1970s, our family was huge prior to us engaging in the camper experience. We were growing leaps and bounds, and we were blessed with five living generations on earth during that time. We were blessed with five living generations again before my beloved mother, Mrs. Elizabeth Irby passed from this world nearly five years ago, in November 2019. All of the pictures that I have taken, developed, and shared throughout time showcases the spectacular times we had while camping with my family. Those times were fabulous and memorable, and we'll talk about them for years to come.

    Heck, it's 2024, and I am writing about the days when I used to camp out with my family! Believe it or not, I remember that our first camping trip down in the country was an adventure that I'll never forget! We had to pitch our tents for shelter. Those who came down unprepared for camping had to sleep under the stars either on the hard ground on a blanket, in their lawn chair, or on a cot, while the rest of us got ready for the comfortable sleeping bag experience of a lifetime. We got cozy and watched the sparks of flames spit and shoot up out of the split fire barrels that gave light for us to see and find our way to the outhouse in the absolute darkness of the midnight sky hovering over us. There were a few Rhode Island Reds still wandering the grounds, so I knew either the coop had been closed, or these ordinary barnyard birds were not bright! We were down in the country in the woods where wildlife lived, and our chickens went to bed early. Apparently, the lifestyle of closing the chickens up in the coop at night has changed since I used to put them up for the night when I was a child. Rather, it has become obsolete, or these couple of ordinary barnyard birds are just different and used to being around people. When I was growing up and stayed down in the country with my Great Aunt Janice and Uncle Palmer, at Great Grandmother's and Great Grandfather's, they had two mixed Belgian shepherd dogs, Jack and Spam. Brownie was Aunt Janice's and Uncle Palmer's pet, and she would later join Jack and Spam on the land in years to come. We were surprised to find that my Great Uncle had several Doberman Pinschers in the backyard caged and held on really thick long chains. They were huge and had BIG LOUD BARKS! I was concerned about having to use the outhouse, so I came prepared with a personal potty and plenty of H20 to flush when necessary! I never used the outhouse as a child at night. I knew that I was not going down there in that darkness. Furthermore, D-ran and his brother were huge dogs, and their loud barking was too much for me.

I had to admit to myself, these were the first dogs that ever frightened me. I exhaled and went on about my business and finished pitching my tent as we were gearing up for our first camping adventure under the stars and fully moonlit night. All of the money that we collected from our yard sales allowed us to have a grand old time. Most of us pitched our tents with the music playing from my recorded tapes, foods were cooking on split barrels, wine and beer was chilling in the coolers, and our little cousins were running around crying because a few of the chickens were still free ranging and running all over the campsite. Our first camping experience was so great because our family participated in so many activities together. A few of my aunts, including my mom, and uncles were yard sale Queens and Kings. They knew exactly where to go to get the best items at the best prices. Throughout our camping years and adventures, during one of our camping extravaganzas, BIG HILARY was erected, and it became our DISCO spot! Hilary was now the place where we jam whatever weekend we were down in the country! Of course, I was the DJ. All of the top tunes that I had recorded from my collection later filled the night air, as we danced the night away. I played some of the best music that any DJ could have anywhere. As time went on, we started aging and began to leave each other through a natural form of passing through this world, and our family generational groups began to drop off. Less of the younger family members seemed interested in maintaining the camping experience and showing up. So, after close to 15 years or so, our camping adventure came to a halt.

Chapter 5
Beautifully Stained Leaves

The making of a beautiful life…

The Big Fight

During the rock & roll, disco and go-go eras, I used to dance and sing downtown at the Chez Maurice, Wilson's Ranch House, Hollywood, and other spots to earn extra money to pay my bills and live the lifestyle that I had come to know and enjoy. I had discovered my newfound young freedom and independence of living. It was exciting and fun! So to avoid having to drive all of the way back home so late at night, I had a key to a friend's home where I could crash and stay over when necessary. On this particular night, I used my spare key to crash at my friend's home. When I opened the front door, there were fists, shoes, and feet flying, along with name calling that I had never heard before! I shouted, "Stop! Stop! What in the hell are y'all fighting about?" Zenia and her husband were tenants of my friend's home. Unfortunately, I had entered what I had always known to have been a safe spot to dwell when I needed. This time, however, it was extremely different – downright scary to be honest! I had walked into a space where a couple was having a nasty name calling argument, and objects that could hurt were flying all around the room. After I ducked a couple of blows and an ashtray, I said, "Stop it! Stop it now before somebody gets hurt!" Then it dawned on me. Zenia is pregnant, and she and her husband are behaving like two completely irresponsible human beings. Having another baby could not be a good decision. I was right! I started asking questions. I said, "Just why in the heck are y'all fighting and calling each other these horrible names? Are you not pregnant again?" Zenia said, "Yes. "That's what this is all about." I said, "What in the heck do you mean?" Chuck jumps up and screams, "I told her that we cannot afford to have any more children, and she keeps getting pregnant." By now, I walked pass them, as they had lowered their voices. So, I get ready to go up to the spare bedroom and to go to bed because I really don't feel like driving back to my apartment because it was so late. Also, I don't want to leave Zenia alone with Chuck while he was expressing and showcasing his dark side.

On my way up the stairs in walks Zandra, a nurse practitioner who owns the property. We speak and she says, "Hey everybody. Zelda, I know why you are here." She continues. "Zenia, why are you and Chuck up so late? It is going on 3:00 in the morning, and why do both of you appear to be out of breath looking like you just finished running a marathon or been in a fight?" By this time, I had taken a seat on the steps and started listening to how the three of them were planning to resolve the matter because I knew Zandra was not going to have them messing up and fighting in her house. Zandra had recently left an abusive relationship, and she was not going to allow that negative energy from anyone ever again in her environment – friend or foe. Zandra looked up at me and started quizzing me on what was happening. Now, I have had to jump down the stairs to help support Zandra and Zenia because Chuck started screaming out loud again, swinging his large fists around in the air, kicking furniture over with his big stinky, corn, bunion, crusty feet, and simply raising hell all over again! This time, it appeared he had become annoyed because Zandra said to Zenia and Chuck, "Y'all don't have to be getting pissed off with each other about having any more children now because the law of the land has been passed." Chuck said, "What are you talking about Zandra?" She says, "I know that I have to keep up with these rules and regulation changes because I work in the healthcare industry. From now on, families, men, and women who cannot afford to increase their families, or for whatever reason, can now be in a safe setting because Roe versus Wade has become a landmark decision by the highest court in the land. The Supreme Court ruled that the Constitution of the United States generally protected a right to have an abortion." Unfortunately, or fortunately, Zenia starts to cry. I really was not sure why. It could have been because she might have been relieved somehow or the other that her husband Chuck had finally left the room and went down the hall to go to bed. Or, it could have been because she was sad thinking about not having another child because they could not afford to take care of another human being.

Dark Alley

For whatever reason, Zenia starting to cry, her sadness, and the awful fight between she and her husband took me back into time to a place in my really young life. I tapped into a sad memory and acknowledged, once again, before Roe versus Wade was passed in 1973, the right to an abortion was illegal. I recalled a couple of really dark times in my life when I got out of the car at the corner, walked down into those dark alleyways without a friend or any assistance to meet up with a complete stranger, get undressed, and lay out on a wooden picnic like table with only a candle burning down low towards the floor area. Another unknown individual who was masked would approach me with cold, but hopefully sterilized instruments in hand, to interrupt a life from entering into the world. I was so afraid, young, and I knew that if I had died, my parents would have been pissed with me for not telling them. But I just couldn't tell them because all I ever heard from both of them my entire upbringing was, "You had better NOT bring any babies into this house." Where I lived, in my headspace, that meant do not bring any babies into their home. Of course, I had a few close girlfriends my age who were going through similar situations. Some had their babies, some were simply sent away and never returned to the area, and some were never seen again. Unfortunately, a few of them died of poverty and died alone because no one cared or gave a damn about them, period! Regardless, that was an awful time in my life, and every day that I live, I regret ever getting up onto that table. Today, I am one of the blessed ones because I am still here now sharing with you what happened to me 50 plus years ago prior to Roe v. Wade becoming the LAW OF THE LAND! Now women are dying all over again because it was overturned! WHY????

To get my mind off the matter, I went on a boat ride a couple weeks later and had to be rushed to emergency because I started hemorrhaging. My soul and spirit from that moment had been pierced forever more, and I believed that I would live and God had forgiven me. I learned how to forgive myself and live the best life that continues today, through the love, grace, and peace of the Lord! Fortunately, for the love and blessings of God and the universe, Zenia and Chuck increased their family by having a set of twins – a girl who they named after me and a son named Zack. We all came to realize one way or another in our lifetime, births and deaths can change how we decide to live our lives. When Zenia passed from this world, Chuck appeared to be happy and better off with having all of his children around him upon losing their beloved mother. Chuck realized that he was a blessed man. He watched his children grow up and become decent and successful citizens. Later on, in his life, he met, loved, and married another woman. As life is for the living, Chuck would not be alone again until it was time for his trip around the sun to be interrupted by the loving power source and grace of God.

Memorial Day Weekend

I had received a telephone call from Leed's dress shop to pick up my clothing. A notice had also come in the mail that same day to pick up lay-a-way merchandise from my shoe store, I. Miller's. After receiving these messages, I got in my car and flew downtown, parked my car, stopped at Blue Mirror to get a huge and delicious slice of strawberry shortcake and a pastrami sandwich and went down the street to pick up my lay-a-way items. I was preparing for a fabulously planned Memorial Day weekend. When I got back home, I found these gorgeous white duck pants that I had forgotten I had selected for this event and a really cute top with multi-color sandals to match. As I was getting my clothes on, my little black C&P short cord telephone starts ringing off the hook. Back in the day, I had the wheels, so I would pick up my friends so we could attend major annual events throughout the DMV. For this particular holiday weekend, I would not be hanging out with my girls because I had been going out with this guy on a regular basis, and we had made plans to be together for the upcoming Memorial Day weekend. I believe we were trying to get to know each other a little better.

I had noticed on previous holidays he would not always be available, but for this particular holiday he was. So, we made plans to attend one of the major cookout events, and I was picking him up. I didn't mind because I had been to his apartment many times before, and he had been to mine as well. On my way out the door, my phone rang, and it was him. He told me that something had come up, and he was unable to attend the cookout. I asked him if he was sick and he said NO. "I'm just not having a good day." The tone in his voice was low energy and pathetic sounding. I said to him, "Well I am sorry that you're having a bad day. Let me come anyway to brighten you up." He said,

"NO." I said, "Okay, but I was really looking forward to seeing you today." We hung up the telephone from talking to each other. I picked up my phone and called one of my girls, telling her about what had happened. I went to pick her up, and we attended the cookout and had a ball as usual. Of course, we didn't have cell phones at the time, so we had fewer interruptions while meeting and talking to strangers along the way.

The cookout area was huge, and people were all over the place. Food and drinks were everywhere, and the music was blasting beautifully. We started to jam. My girlfriend said, "I hate to bring this up, but I believe I see your friend over by the fence with another girl." I said, "WHERE?" She said, "Over there." When I turned my head, I couldn't believe my eyes. There he was standing there with another girl. I thought to myself that she must be his sister, aunt, a coworker, an old friend – because she couldn't be his daughter or his momma. I took a really deep breath before I decided how I was going to handle and resolve this particular situation. By now, I have decided to walk over and get closer to their space to see if I can hear anything that he should not be saying to her that would cause me to react. I get closer, and she calls out my name. "Hi, Zelda." I said, "Who are you?" She said, "I love your records, and that playboy pink Mustang with that black vinyl roof you drive is groovy!" I said, to myself, *"Who in the hell is this person, and where did she ever come from?"* He asks, "Y'all know each other?" and I say, "NO." I told him that we need to talk. She politely stepped away, and he and I had a brief discussion. Come to find out, they are married, but separated, and she has the children living in another state. However, she comes from a family of veterans, and she was in town in Virginia to place flags on her father's and grandfather's grave sites because they were fallen soldiers. He asked me if I would forgive him for the rest of the day, to see her off and that we would get together later on in the evening over at his apartment. I agreed, and my girlfriend and I went back over to be with our friends and enjoyed the rest of the festivities at the cookout. By now, it's getting late, and the sun is going down. He comes over to tell me that he will see me in a couple of hours if I were still willing to come by, and of course, I told him that I would be over after I had dropped off my girlfriend to her boyfriend's spot because he had to work Memorial Day weekend. After I dropped her off, I drove all of the way back across town to his apartment. I could not believe what I saw when I turned the key and walked into his apartment. Yep! I had a key to his spot. He had a key to mine. Back in the day, we used to share keys. However, when I got to his apartment, after all of the previous events of that day, it would simply knock your socks off. When I saw what had occurred, I was completely and absolutely blown from the bottom floor of the ocean. Believe it or not, when I entered his apartment Smokey Robinson's record, "Cruisin" was playing. There were warm aromas of incense traveling and floating through the joint, lots of pleasurable sexual noises being made, and his uncovered naked butt was going up and down like it was on a seesaw! I started flipping the light switch up and down like his butt was going. Both of them grabbed for the sheet like you see in the movies after being caught, and with their mouths and eyes now wide open, they looked like two teenagers who had been caught by a parent. I looked at them for a second, turned and got the hell out of dodge. By now he's jumped out of the bed to chase me down the hallway. I threw the key at him, and told him not to ever call me again. Three days later, he showed up at the desk of my good government job questioning me about vandalism to his brand-new Porsche-911. I told him the only information that I could share with him: I had heard he had been in a bad accident, but that he had not suffered any serious injuries. Because the car was a total loss, overhauling the damages would include a paint job.

4th of July Weekend

After I hung up the telephone from talking with K-Nel, I ran down the hall and went out into the hot weather, and jumped into my 1965 playboy pink with black vinyl roof Mustang to go see what was happening to my friend. I knocked on K-Nel's apartment door, and he answered it. He was pissed about something. I said, "What's wrong now K-Nel?" He replied, "I cannot believe that she has put me down after all that we have been through." When I saw the state of mind he was in, I knew that I was in for the long haul despite the fact that it's July 4th, and I have got plans to celebrate with friends and be with my boyfriend. Anyway, K-Nel goes back into his bedroom, and I asked him if he wanted me to fix his lunch because I had to be leaving soon. By now, he has come out into the living space, takes a seat on that big brown leather sofa and starts crying. I am in shock because I have never seen him cry – or any grown man – cry like that before. I asked him if he could share what was happening between him and Birdie, his girlfriend who lived in Baltimore. He hesitated, so I just jumped in and said to him, "Did she catch you cheating on her again?" He said, "What do you think?" So, I said, "From what I remember, she told you in front of me and everyone else y'all know that if she caught you cheating on her again, it would be over. Damn, K-Nel, I'm so sorry brotherman. It sounds like she means it this time around because y'all have been together for five years, and you kept missing the deadline to give her that ring you kept promising her with a proposal of marriage." K-Nel lit up a joint and offered me a hit. I turned him down because I would be leaving soon, and I had to drive a bit of distance to meet up with my boyfriend. I was not going to miss the opportunity of having drinks and sharing a joint or two with him. There's a knock at the door. K-Nel asks me to answer the door, and there's Zocora, a friend of K-Nel's standing at the door with her precious little black poodle, named Pepper. She enters the apartment asking where K-Nel is. I holla out to K-Nel to let him know that she is in the living room.

I hear them having a conversation about her asking him to keep Pepper so she can meet up with her boyfriend and attend a cookout. Zocora tells K-Nel that she heard about his break-up with Birdie and that she was sorry that it happened.

K-Nel tells Zocora to sit down on the sofa and take a deep breath because he had some bad news for her. Zocora stands up immediately and says, "What bad news are you talking about?" K-Nel tells her to sit down, and he delivers the bad news. I was ready to leave after the announcement because I knew that she was going to raise hell, and I was right. I snatched up the keys to my car, and I heard K-Nel say, "Can you sit with her for a minute? I have got to make a phone call and try to get Birdie to forgive me one more time." I told him good luck with that! After K-Nel delivered the bad news to Zocora – that her boyfriend had left town last night on a flight to the West Coast – I saw Zocora pick up one of K-Nel's joints off of the table and fire it up! All of a sudden, she stood up and kicked in the floor model Motorola TV with her bare foot and began to pick stuff up and throw it against the wall and around the room. I knew that I was in danger when I had to duck a couple of objects from hitting me, as Zocora was totally out of control.

K-Nel came into the room yelling, "What in the hell is going on?" I told him that Zocora had smoked one of his joints, and he said, "Damn, she can't smoke what I smoke because it's laced." I said, "Laced with what?" The next thing I knew, she had stabbed K-Nel, and then I dialed 911 to tell police what was happening. They dispatched a car and ambulance to K-Nel's apartment. I was glad to have called the police at the time I did because I didn't want to become a part of a murder scene in the making. Blood was everywhere, and K-Nel was trying his best to hold Zocora, but she was totally out of control and had simply gone buck-wild. I finally got close enough to Zocora and slapped her down, and she fell onto the leather sofa. The police and EMTs arrived, and they were knocking on the door. I let the emergency team in because K-Nel was bleeding and sitting on Zocora to keep her from moving anymore until the emergency team could assist. I believed she was already out from my slap. All of her kicking, screaming, and smoking the laced joint was the result of the bad news she had previously heard about her boyfriend. A mental breakdown came about, and she had to accept that she had been cheated on by the man she claimed to love.

By now, the emergency team was taking a look at K-Nel's stab wounds. From what I could see, he and Zocora both were put into the ambulance and taken to Providence Hospital. I followed the ambulance to the hospital and waited in the visitors' lounge for the doctor to share the findings of K-Nel's injuries and to see if there was any news about Zocora. I had heard one of the EMTs say, "The woman should be taken up to the psychiatric area." The map on the wall displayed the different locations and departments at Providence Hospital, and the psych ward was on the ninth floor. I knew that I would have to take K-Nel home, so I waited for him and embraced the fact that my July 4th activities with my boyfriend had been shot straight to hell. The doctor came out and said that K-Nel would be coming out from the emergency room soon, that his injury from the stabbing was not severe, and that he would be alright. I took a chance and asked the doctor if he knew how Zocora was doing. I was surprised when the doctor started running off at the mouth about how mentally deranged and unstable she was to the point where the team in the emergency room had to restrain her using a straitjacket. The medical team didn't want her to further hurt herself. Accordingly, today, I learned the method of using a straitjacket to restrain human beings ended back in the 1950s, despite some institutions continuing to use them until the late 20th century. However, research provides that straitjackets are considered outdated and inhumane, and they have been replaced with other means to halt patients from further injuring themselves or others who could be in the line of danger.

Finally, K-Nel was released from the hospital, and l took him home. Then I went on about my merry way to meet up with my boyfriend, and we enjoyed what was left of that July 4th holiday weekend. K-Nel told me later that Birdie had forgiven him again, that he was going to pop the question and ask her to marry him, and he invited me to their special event. He also shared that he had later learned that Zocora survived the betrayal of her boyfriend leaving her for a west coast woman. Zocora had returned to her corporate job and got married several years later to a wonderful older gentleman, and they had three children: two girls and one boy – now all grown up with families of their own. Unfortunately, Zocora's husband passed from this world before their children graduated from high school, but they now have their own families and Zocora is a happy grandmother. K-Nel told me that he was blessed to serve as godfather to all of Zocora's children.

Chapter 6
Tea Time

The time of my life...

Trip to South Africa

One morning me and one of my dearest friends, Mimi McDaniels (RIP), were talking on our landline telephones and the topic of travel arose. She started telling me that she, her sister, and brother-in-law, Bill (RIP), were seriously looking at a trip to South Africa. I told Mimi that if she goes on that trip, I would be her roommate if she needed one. In our next conversation later that same week, it was confirmed we were going to travel to South Africa. It was one of the best trips that I have taken so far in my lifetime. Before we actually left America for our Europe and South Africa experience, we had an initial meet and greet and met several times afterwards with the entire group of individuals who were going on the trip. The group included Dr. Betty (RIP), who sponsored the trip along with her traveling partner Greg, of Harvey World Travel. In the early morning of March 4, 2003, our group (16 of us) had arrived at Dulles airport to begin our overseas adventure. We bowed our heads in prayer and asked God to keep our plane safe in the sky as it crossed the seas of the Atlantic Ocean. We also asked to be safe from the beginning of our trip until we returned home two days before the Iraq War started. I had never flown first class on British Airways before! The service was top shelf, with all of the bells and whistles! The flight attendants were on their mark during the entire time of the trip. The first leg of our trip was 10 hours to London. Please know that I was grateful to get off that plane, despite all the good food dishes and snacks, delicious drinks, and comfortable accommodations. We stayed in London for a couple days and went shopping at the most famous department store in the world – Harrods – where the iconic late Victorian facade dominates the busy Kensington thoroughfare. I purchased a set of Queen Elizabeth champagne flutes and a pair of kid leather gloves. When I got up to the counter to pay, I thought that I was going to pass out because of how much the items cost.

After that experience, we found a quaint little pub and had lots of beer and fish and chip dishes. Overall, my experience of the food in London did not make my taste buds happy. We did a lot of sightseeing like most folks do when they travel, and I was surprised to see how green the grass was in London. It was awfully pretty and bright green everywhere we went. My best guess is maybe because it's so foggy. I found it interesting to have learned that London has so many churches, and most Brits do not even attend church. Of course, we went to Westminster Abbey and saw the changing of the guard, which was *kool*. I took a lot of pictures and shared them with Mimi and some people who were in our group after I got back because this trip was a once in a lifetime trip for most. We got back to our hotel, had a party, and continued celebrating ourselves and the good life we were living. It was time to go back to the airport. We were on to Durban – next stop Johannesburg, South Africa and Cape Town.

Durban was a beautiful place to visit, but I found it unique that the population of Durban is made up of Indians from the country of India. Finally, we arrived in Johannesburg, South Africa, in the dark of night. After we got checked into our hotel, we said goodnight, had a night cap, and went to our suites. The next morning, Dr. Betty met us for breakfast to share the itinerary for the day. Upon boarding our coach, the driver and curators made their statements, and we were off to our day's activities. While we were driving through the town of Johannesburg, it was quite dismal and gloomy looking, and I saw lots of poverty. During one of our many sightseeing adventures, we stopped at one of the many parks – the Kruger National Park – where we saw a group of men sitting around the Paul Kruger statue, rocking back and forward in protest of housing and employment discrimination, despite apartheid ending in 1994. Black people got to vote in a new government, and Nelson Mandela was inaugurated as President, May 10, 1994. His term as President ended on June 14, 1999. Fortunately, for us, Dr. Betty was our guide who sponsored our trip. She was raised by parents who were missionaries. According to her, she lived in lots of different places throughout the world, including Africa. During her educational experiences, she taught in various South African schools during apartheid. While the struggle of freedom was underway, she met Nelson and Winnie Mandela and Desmond Tutu, The Most Reverend, of St. George Cathedral, Cape Town. Desmond Tutu was an Anglican

Bishop and Theologian known for his participation as an anti-apartheid and human rights activist. Our visit to St. George was powerful because we took some liberties for sweet memories for my upcoming scrapbooking of my South Africa experience. I wanted to share this experience with others once I completed the project. I quickly removed the rope from The Most Reverend Desmond Tutu's chair and got my picture taken. There was a group of people on the other side of the cathedral having a conversation about HIV-AIDS. I ventured over to hear details, and I was asked to not ask so many questions because talking about HIV-AIDS was still taboo in South Africa at that time.

My favorite trip was to South Africa. I remember it like it was yesterday, although I traveled there some 21 years ago and was blessed to return the day the Iraq war started. George Bush was the President of America. I can talk about South Africa until the day I die. It was a trip of a lifetime. I would love to go back, but the only problem is I would not want to return to America with all of the unrest that is happening in our politics today. I would really consider exploring the idea of living someplace else. Now I know what my mother and father meant when they were raising me and my brothers to be careful, and that no matter where we went in our lives, to be mindful that the world is a beautiful place, but it is the people in it who make it a scary place. So be wise and look both ways before crossing any street anywhere! Every now and again, I pull my bucket list out and take a peek at it because I really want to visit Tanzania to see Mountain Kilimanjaro. I also want to walk through Serengeti National Park and maybe see or at least hear the migration of the animals soon. But I am now concerned about the unrest throughout the entire globe. It may not be safe to journey from the land of milk and honey to a foreign country for any reason, bucket list or not. So, I had better stay put because nowadays, I believe the leadership across the globe have caused me to acknowledge the world is a scary place no matter where you live or visit.

When we landed in South Africa, it was night, and we were extremely tired and ready for some real rest because our itinerary was packed with planned and exciting adventures throughout our entire trip. The next morning, after our arrival, the sixteen of us met Dr. Betty and her Harvey Travel team for breakfast. We got on the coach, and off we went to the bush, as they called it. We had a wonderful curator on our coach, and he was a friend of Dr. Betty's. He was a native of South Africa. As we rode through some of the unpaved streets and desolate areas in Johannesburg, we saw poverty peeking out all over the place. The scene began to change, somewhat, as we came upon a little city called Soweto. The people were out in the streets, and children were running towards us as we departed the coach. A certain type of transportation vehicle transporting sightseers is called a BUS in the United States, but in South Africa, that type of vehicle is called a COACH, and the driver will remind you not to call it a bus! We stopped for lunch at a restaurant called Wandie's in the Township of Soweto. I was amazed to see so many people dressed in different garb or outfits, if you will, from all over the world waiting to get a seat for their meal in this dive! It was truly a dive! But my goodness, the food was simply delicious! As we stood out front waiting to get into the joint, the towns folks were coming up to us asking us to shoot them! I was wondering why they were asking us to shoot them. I heard one towns person respond and say, "We simply want you to take our picture." Of course, I had lost my mind, so I started taking pictures of everyone who I believed was from Soweto. It was a fun time until it was time to board the coach. About

10 children started running toward us, shouting, "Please mam, please mam, take me with you. I will not give you any trouble, I promise you, I am a good boy."

At that moment, I lost it all, and one of my traveling partners became afraid. After I comforted her, she boarded the coach. Then I turned my attention back to the little guy and explained to him why I could not take him home with me. He was so dirty. It simply broke my heart. I wanted to give him the shawl I was carrying to keep me warm had the weather changed. At that time, I had become saddened myself because I could not do anything to help that child and his friends who were sure enough living in deep poverty! After I gave them some money, and whatever else was in my purse, I just got back on the coach and started boo-hooing and telling GOD that I will never complain about anything ever again in my life. Now all of us were back on the coach and headed back to Shamba Village Hotel. We were told in the very beginning of our stay to keep the windows closed to keep monkeys from coming to the visit. Of course, I didn't pay any attention to the command. I opened my barred windows and who came to visit us shortly thereafter was a monkey who I immediately named Micky's Monkey after one of Smokey Robinson's hit records. He did not stay at the window long because the grounds people had means to deter the monkeys from hanging around. I have to admit it was fun seeing a monkey up close and personal because I had never in my life ever been that close to a real monkey before. It was time for dinner, and every meal that I ate throughout my South African adventure was exceptionally delicious! Before leaving Soweto, we went to church, and it was a special visitation including a special musical presentation by children and townspeople. It was another joyous occasion in the celebration of my life with friends and absolute strangers from around the world.

Now we're back at the airport because we're flying to Durban to sightsee, to witness the happenings in that township, and to learn that there are many Indians from the country of India who prefer living and enjoying their lives and time under Durban rule. The food was out of this world, and the people were happy and kind. Our hotel was gorgeous! The party that Craig of Harvey World Travel had for us was outstanding. Now we're headed to Cape Town – a place in which I knew my blood pressure would rise despite the educational experience we would come away with – an educational experience that would help to lower my level of militance. I realized I had prepared myself for this journey to actually stand on the grounds of and be in the place where former prisoner, Nelson Mandela, was the first African man to become President after the collapse of apartheid in South Africa. Once on board of the yacht that took us over to Robben Island, it was so quiet you could hear a kitten pee on cotton. Shortly after getting off the MAKANA yacht, we were escorted around the island and introduced to the curator who had also been in prison with President Mandela. We got firsthand, up close and personal information about some of the happenings during the Mandela era. I remember my heart racing when the curator was sharing information about how the prisoners were treated and how so many went blind due to the sun shining down on the salt mines as the prisoners beat the rock to gravel. Some died from heat exhaustion, due to not being given water to drink! On several occasions, I had to step away from the group because the information the curator had shared was so DAMN HARSH and PAINFUL to hear! We actually had one individual from another group share our time and space during our tour of the island, and her remarks shocked us all.

She challenged the curator, and said out loud, "I DON'T BELIEVE ANY OF THESE THINGS HAPPENED HERE TO THESE PRISONERS!" My blood was in full boil mode, and I thought that I was going to pass out!! After her comments, I backed away from the groups and almost missed the walk-through President Mandela's cell. The curator was kind and generous enough with his time and attention to allow me to come back, and he walked me through President Mandela's cell one-on-one! On the way back to the MAKANA yacht, I noticed there were a few other travelers who were from both groups that were huddled up together because what they had just witnessed made them just as sick as it had made me. Hearing what the curator shared and seeing with our own eyes how the prisoners had lived through the apartheid era of South Africa was hard to dispel.

Our itinerary was packed with fantastic sightseeing adventures every day. Our ride in the sky trolley up to "Table Mountain" was extraordinary. In all of my days, I never dreamed that I would ever venture and get on one of these aerial tramway lifts which used one or two stationary ropes for support while a third moving rope provided propulsion. Once we were on top of the mountain, I was thrilled. The mountain was so flat, and its views were simply breathtaking. There were the cute little Dassie mountain rodents that were all over the place, but they were not annoying. My best guess is that the cute little hind leg standing mammals had become accustomed to human beings who temporarily invaded their home space on the mountain, as opposed to us having to get accustomed to them during the tour. The Dassie share the mountain with lizards, tortoises, and a rare endemic species of amphibian that is only found on Table Mountain – the ghost frog. The trip we took over the Atlantic to see the seals was extremely eventful. I had gotten on a small boat on this particular morning, knowing that I knew better than to be getting on any boat because I cannot do the east and west ride on boats because of my inner ear issue. But I could not go all the way to South Africa and NOT complete the itinerary from start to finish.

    So, there I was with the rest of the group. We boarded a boat that had not left the dock yet, but it was rocking and reeling like a warped record on a turntable with a bad needle. The Atlantic Ocean was mean that morning, and I felt my heart begin to jump and my stomach was in real bad shape! By this time, some of my fellow travelers were getting sick and throwing up on each other. It was not a pretty sight by any means. Then all of a sudden, we hit a wave or a wave hit us, and my roommate, Mimi (RIP), popped up off the bench and fell down into the stairway. The beads on her bracelet were everywhere. I picked them up because I knew that particular bracelet was special to her. I gathered as many as I could find and later told her that I had gathered them and she said, "I don't want them, you keep 'em." I put them in one of three scrapbooks that I made from my South Africa adventures. I miss my Mimi to this day. She went home to be a part of the heavenly host in 2007. Mimi, this one is for you, Darling. Our visit into the halls of Parliament was very special because it was different to see so many Black people in power of their own government. This was completely opposite of apartheid. Visiting the Zulu Village was really fantastic because we made the discovery that Zulu people are rich and live very well in their surrounding communities – completely unlike what is polarized in the media. One of the meals we had for breakfast included an ostrich egg, and from that one egg, the chef made 21 omelets! Simply delicioso!! As we were winding down from our exciting adventures of South Africa, Dr. Betty (RIP) called us together for a fabulous dinner, and she shared more stories with us about the time she lived and taught school in South Africa. She told us how she had become close friends with Nelson and Winnie Mandela and the great powers and struggles of the country at the time. I was so privileged to have been in Mr. Mandela's office. I sat in his chair and looked out into one of the most gorgeous gardens that I had ever seen in my life.

  During Dr. Betty's storytelling time, she begged our pardon and asked us to forgive her for her mishap – leaving her attaché case behind on the coach when she had continued to remind us to not leave anything on the coach when unoccupied because people from outside can sometimes get onto the coach and steal stuff. Unfortunately, she left stuff on the coach when it was unoccupied, and our information – with the exception of our passports – was stolen. We missed a half day of planned activities because we had to go downtown with her to obtain our paperwork. After several hours had passed, we were all back into the groove, and all of the paperwork that had been stolen from Dr. Betty's attaché case had now been duplicated and returned. I left South Africa with sweet and sour memories to last me a lifetime. Who knew that I would ever be taking time out to write and share my experiences with others who buy and read my warm, heartfelt green tea leaves stories of South Africa. My other favorite trips were to Paris, Spain, Rome, England, Aruba, Turks and Caicos, and places in the Caribbean.

Mother's Day

It's Mother's Day, May 12, 2024, and I am at home feeling extremely blessed because I'm in good health, able to keep a roof over my head, clothes on my back, and eat whatever foods I like – along with consuming libations of my choice. I received many phone calls, text messages, and cards from my daughter and friends over time. I remember back in the day when I used to plan Mother's Day activities for the entire family to engage in and enjoy. One even included a book signing. In softer moments of teatime, I learned a fact that would put me on an ongoing journey that finally came to an end. I learned if you liked or loved the sound of a particular individual's voice in your life who passed from this world, keep in mind that once that individual passes and transitions, they take their personal sound of their voice with them back up to the universe, stardust, or heavenly space, and we here on earth can never hear the sweet sounds of their voices ever again. My best advice to you if you want to hold on to and hear the sound of the voices of people who you liked or loved again, is to be sure that you take time out to record the sound of their voice on a device. Otherwise, please know that you will never ever be able to replicate the sound of their voice in your headspace ever again – no matter what you do. Trust me on this one. I have tried it so many times. Those voices are now with the heavenly host!

  Also know that in my many climbs to reach the top and stand on the mountain, sometimes my trips were complete falls to the ground -- falls with blood stains still left behind in the places I fell to mark my fall. Bruises and scars are reminders to take different paths and directions, but to keep the dream alive and reach the goal at the end of whatever day that brings closure to realizing the achievement was complete. Remember the lyrics from the song about that little ant who had high hopes – high apple pie in the sky hopes because we all know that an ant cannot ever move a rubber tree. I pray that you walk away from reading my book and appreciate that death can't be that much. Rather, appreciate that living is the daily challenge we all face until God sends his text that we will not be able to ignore. Smooches.

The End

An awful thing happened to me yesterday. I went to Jersey Mike's to get a sub and chips. Most folks who purchase food from Jersey Mike's know if you sign up for their special program you get points, and you eventually can get a free any size sub that matches the points that you have collected. Since yesterday was a day for me to get a FREE sub, I decided to get a soda, and I rarely ever drink soda. I reached for a small cup, and then I decided to get a medium size drink. I pressed the button for a lemon/lime Starry drink. I took a swig of the soda, and everything that I knew was real in this world had gone away.

Meaning, I began to gasp for air because I could not breathe, and I reached for the countertop to brace myself because I felt like I was falling. Then all of a sudden, a wonderful human being named Jason (daughter Stella, 7 years old) came to my rescue. While gasping for breath, Jason took my hat off of my head and started fanning me, and I was trying to go to sleep. Then Jason introduced me to his little girl, Stella. He then started asking me to stay with him until the ambulance arrived. I remember trying to still go to sleep. Jason was not having it! Before I knew it, he was pressing on my face and turning my head and repeatedly calling out my name, "Zelda, Zelda, please stay with me. The guys are on their way!"

By now, I am really out of it because I knew that I had an allergic reaction to whatever preservatives were in that soda. They had negatively affected my health. Then I realized that I had urinated on myself in public, but there was nothing that I could do about it! Once the EMTs arrived, one of them took my pressure, started asking me questions, and they did their rescue thing. I didn't want to go to the emergency room, but I went anyway. That was another entirely awful experience! For those of you who have ever been in an emergency room at any hospital, you know exactly what I am talking about. I will not bore you to tears with that one! But I do pray that one day I will see Jason and his little daughter again because I would like to thank Jason for catching me and preventing me from falling to the floor and hitting my head.

I believe we all have guardian angels surrounding us every day! Jason was mine yesterday, and I appreciate the spiritual energy that allowed him to serve me when I needed help. After all of the tea that I have spilled over time, including up to now, I know from life experiences that everyone's tea party has not necessarily been good! But we are here on earth as gifts to each other, and I am hopeful that one day we will come to know and appreciate that there is no better calling than to serve another human being. I am of the opinion that serving another human being can be as easy as pouring a cup of tea and sharing in a good and healthy conversation with full intentions to use each other in a loving, kind, and respectful manner – not misuse each other with intent to harm, hurt, disrespect, or betray.

After all is said and done, sacrificing my own suicide from back in the day, was a blind blessing. Furthermore, I had a child to raise, love, and guide through the true blessings of God's grace, love, and peace. Her journey into my life mattered, which caused me to honor that the reward of living was so much better than choosing to leave the planet prematurely. It wasn't for me to leave her behind for someone else to step up to a responsibility that I almost ignored. I discovered sooner than later through the peace, love, and grace of GOD that ALL of the pain and misery I endured was worth it in the preparation of me embracing my blessings of the future and of every day the good Lord would send me after that.

My dear reader, now that you have read my first book, I pray that you walk away with an appreciation and understanding to accept my approach as I see it. I have found joy spilling my tea. It is a burden lifted, and it causes my living spirit to feel happy, free, and healthy – mentally and physically. So, when a girl decides to be a legend, embrace her!!

My Girls & Lifelong Friendships

Cassandra A. Herbert McMorris, Ma & Pa Herbert (RIP) & Herbert Family, Gregory F. Proctor, Rosetta G. Irby, Darlene V. Irby,

Brenda S. Dew, Marlo D. Crawford, Zelda D. Holmon, Betty B. Butler, Patricia B. Robinson, Sandra H. & Reginald Handon, Fannie Jo Wynn Tate (RIP), Gwendolyn J. Thompson, Mikie Hoffman (RIP), Mae Homans, Leon & Gerri Thomas, Donna Robinson, Rosalyn O. C. Moore, Beryl S. & Al-Tony Gilmore, Carolyn & Curtis Byrd (RIP), Marlene C. & Francis Thomas, Delores (RIP) & William Finister, Melayne & Lauren Richards, Kesha & Sean Terry, Tanya Patton & Maurice Coakley, Sweetie Cuzin "Pete" Gladys Thomas & Harry Strother, Jean Robinson White (OBS), Lisa & Mike Lofty, Maceo Bond, Cindi Powell, "DCRL White," Suziane & Anthony Hollins, Carol & Gregory Miller, Kishore & Sriju Rimal, Dr. Brenna Steinberg & Staff, and Marina Seawright who I affectionately called (Grandma Wright). She was a loving, caring, and kind woman to all the neighbors in our hood growing up on 26th Street, Northeast, Washington, District of Columbia. She taught me how to bake a sweet potato pie and make cornbread muffins. Her daughter, Jessie Catherine (Cat) Davis, was like my big sister, and her husband, Nineveh Hudson (Hut) Davis, loved and adored me so much they named their last daughter after me – Zelda, who to this day, I call Little Zee. Their cousin, Jerome

Whitaker, who I adopted as my little play brother, was best friend to my natural blood brother Kenny Boy. Also, thank you to my very special friends, Wanda, Kodjo, and Circa for all of their love and support to me while I was writing my first book!

My First Book

I liked writing as much as I liked singing and painting, but I never took the time nor energy to commit to such a major project as writing an entire book. Furthermore, when I was a child, I did not believe in my heart, mind, and spirit that I had command of the King's language – English – to successfully write an entire book, even though diagramming sentences was one of my favorite things to do in my spare time. Once again, in my personal and challenging life, I was WRONG! But oh, the sun would come out and shine brightly for me when I took it seriously and realized that I did have command of my own language and that I could commit to and discipline myself to write my first book. So that was a real self-lesson, as I was able to read my own "Tea Leaves" from lessons learned!! But after a certain age, life experiences would take me up, down, around corners, bends, and back around different directions again. Soon, I would come to know that these unique life lessons would bring me to a place in my life where I would pump my brakes and exhale. I had finally come to a complete STOP. I took a look around to embrace all attributes and elements like time, commitment, energy, confidence to complete and successfully write my first book, and bring it to market for purchase and to be read – if for no other reason than out of curiosity or for another item checked off of my bucket list!!! While my first book, Spilled Tea Tastes Better: Kools Bittersweet "A Dorell, Adventure, Maybe Baby, and Good Luck to The Lucky Girl," may not ever see daylight or be on the bestseller list or even make one of Oprah's Book Club announcements. I have accomplished one of the many goals that I established for myself when I was a little girl, as well as to have witnessed the force of gravity to forever pull down any face that time and wrinkles are okay. I didn't really know, understand, or have a clue at that time about what the real values of setting goals truly meant. But over time, I have certainly come to know, understand, and appreciate the satisfaction, joy, and fulfillment of what it involves – including the true meaning of what it feels like to be an author, able to share some of my life challenges with you and be happy about it all!

Now that I have completed my first book, I will now have to turn my attention to the bucket list items I have left to see what I can scratch off next to keep myself busy, enjoying, and living my best life that God has given me. I am blessed today – in good health, peace of mind, with a roof over my head, food to eat, and favorite drinks to consume. I have love and compassion for family and friends, and I get to be charitable to those who are less fortunate – four-legged ones included. Thank you, Lord, for Meagan Pinkney. She is one of the most patient human beings I have ever met in my life! TO GOD BE THE GLORY!!!

Author Bio

Zelda was born at Freedman's Hospital and raised in the District of Columbia, Washington. She attended the public school system and went to Woodridge Elementary, Taft Junior High, and McKinley Technical High. Upon graduating from McKinley, she applied to several colleges including Saint Augustine in North Carolina and Ethic College in Flushing New York. She got accepted to both but attended Federal City College, which is now the University of the District of Columbia.

Zelda has one loving daughter, Ms. Allison Elizabeth Irby Vu, one grandson, Master Enzo, and three brothers, Mr. Henry E. Irby, Jr., Mr. Kenneth M. Irby, Sr., and Reverend Kenneth F. Irby. Zelda's parents, her beloved and late father Mr. Henry E. Irby, Sr., passed through from this world 32 years ago, and her beloved and late mother, Mrs. Elizabeth Josephine Irby, transitioned five years ago.

Zelda's federal government career spanned over 31 years of service, including 10 years of private and corporate employment. She also participated and volunteered in many fundraising activities and events in her local and surrounding communities, as well as in federal environments during her youth and adult life. Her volunteer experience with Hospice was heartfelt, stemming from the love, undivided attention, and tenderness that was provided by the staff to her late father many years ago, as well as to her mother before she passed from this life five years ago.

Zelda is finally writing her first book because writing, painting, and singing have always been her passions! Zelda became a recording artist at the tender age of 14 when she formed the singing group, The Dorells. The Dorells included Beverly "Amshatar" Monroe and Renee' Morris Rickman. "Maybe Baby" and "Good Luck to The Lucky Girl" were the two records they recorded as a teenage singing group. Their group appeared on the Teenarama dance party, which was a TV broadcast by WOOK where young black teenagers danced and had a great time after school if their grades allowed.

REMINDER: Be Kind to Animals Too!!

It looked like a rainbow descended to East Church Street. Runners were drenched in bright red and blue, bold green and yellow, and brilliant gold. There were colorful sneakers trimmed with dots and sparkles, and some runners were sporting already damp and dingy tee shirts. All had plastic tags illuminated with large numbers hanging around their necks, showcasing the name of their favorite charity, as they positioned themselves on the asphalt, that I had nicknamed 270 Annex Speedway. It was now blocked off for the annual Frederick, Maryland 5K race, which was one block from my house on a dreary Sunday morning. As the soft rain drops began to splash the grass, sidewalk, and asphalt, thousands of runners were on their way to make their mark in the 5K race with the finish line at the Fairgrounds five miles away. I had to rush back down the sidewalk and get back in the house because Sir Tobi hates the rain. Once he completed his morning dump, we quickly moved back down East Church towards the house to avoid being soaked. Still, I was amazed to see so many people running in the rain for any reason. But to get wet for a charity, bless their hearts, I found myself saluting them as they continued running the race despite the rain that was coming down heavier now than before – rain that was now mixed with their blood, sweat, tears, painful and sore and tight muscles, and limp legs swelling to make it to the finish line with family and friends cheering them on.

  Hours later I was getting ready to fix breakfast, and I could not believe that I was out of eggs as I was prepared to make some scrambled ones with cheese grits and rainbow trout. So, I went to the store. I was surprised but happy to find that East Church Street was open again to traffic, and that I could get out of my complex without having to drive around Robin Hood's Barn to get to the Giant. Unfortunately, on my way back home from the store, I had to slow down on East Church, because I thought I saw a big rock in the street. It was not a rock at all. It was a HUGE ASS TURTLE! Well, I put my flashers on and cars behind me began to stop or go around me. I saw one walker on the right of the sidewalk and another couple coming behind him. The first gentleman was so kind, I wished I had gotten his name. He tried to help, but Ralph was too big and heavy for the gentleman to lift. He kindly said, "I don't want to lose a figure today." I said, "I understand." So, I approached the other couple who were still walking toward me. I told them what was happening, and before I knew it, the young boy, said, "What can I do to help you with this turtle?" I told him that if we do not get Ralph back inside of the fenced-in pond, more than likely, he will get CRUSHED by one of these fast and furious drivers who speed down East Church Street like it is 270 Annex Speedway.

He ran over to pick up the turtle, and I yelled, "Hold one minute. Please, take this sheet and use these gloves to protect your hands." He said, "I got this Miss." I said, "Please, be careful. You do not have to use the sheet if you don't want to, but PLEASE take these gloves." He agreed to use the gloves. He picked up Ralph and put him back over into the fenced-in pond. We hugged each other, shared high fives, PRAISED GOD, and he continued walking with his mother south of East Church Street. I got back in my car and went home and fixed my delicious, scrambled eggs, cheese grits, fish, and other yummy Sunday morning treats, plus I had communion. I keep the gloves in my car because they were my mother's gloves and after her passing, I never took them out of my car. My mother had a dog named Ralph. That may have been the reason why I called our rescue turtle Ralph. I believe every living thing should have a name. Ralph is safe if he decides not to walk up out of the fenced-in pond area again. Turtles have feet, you know. They walk.

Remembering My Aunt Frankie and My Great Aunt Janice

Hey Aunt Frankie. Yesterday, you asked me to send you an email with "things" I remember about our beloved Mrs. Janice Strother Palmer – my Great Aunt Janice!

Listed below for you, as requested, and locked in my heart today and forevermore, are memories I hold dear about my darling Great Aunt Janice. Believe it or not, when I was growing up, I had a few goals in life. One was to become a business owner, make money, get a good job, have children, and take care of my great Aunt Janice all because she was so good, kind, and loving. She cared about me as if I were her own daughter. Today, I think about her, talk about her, and miss her still! Memories of Great Aunt Janice, your mother's only sister, are all so special to me. As previously mentioned, my great Aunt Janice was a "Sweetheart," and I adored her dearly!!! Everybody knows that she loved and cared about her parents, siblings, and other members of our family. Great Aunt Janice had a smile that could melt snow! She was extremely smart and kind to people! In her job and leadership position as an assistant funeral director, her personal and work ethics were always at top shelf! Simply put, she had high standards and valued her relationships with friends and respected people from all walks of life, whether they were rich or poor! She had the grace of a Queen! She was an outstanding businesswoman, secretary, organizer, event planner, and a member of the Eastern Star. As a young girl and into my adult years, I watched her serve folks of her community and help lots of people. She was the right hand to Uncle Palmer at L.P. Palmer Funeral Home, 412 "H" Street, N.E. Washington, D.C. Some might recall her being lowkey, but she was bold, brave, and not afraid of anything or anyone! She was a very kind-spirited and generous human being. She was kind and generous to those she encountered on the streets of Northeast Washington, D.C. – or anywhere for that matter. I recalled many days after a funeral, that she would befriend strangers from off the streets, welcome them upstairs into their living space, and give homeless people a hot meal. She offered them a washcloth and soap to clean up, and on occasion, if the individual looked sick or weak, she would offer them a seat of comfort in the upper front room to take a nap! She could cook just about anything and make it taste yummy and delicious! Great Aunt Janice was a master at canning and preserving any type of vegetable or fruit. I recall months in late October or early November, my daddy, Henry E. Irby, Sr., would take Great Aunt Janice and Great Grandmother sacks of pears he had picked from our pear tree in the backyard of 2909 26th, N.E., Washington, D.C., 20018. He would take the pears down into the country where Great Aunt Janice would wash, clean, and cook the pears, prepare handwritten labels with dates and names, and fill the sterilized mason jars, rubbers, and caps with lots of pears, cloves, and juices for future desserts and other upcoming treats for us to enjoy on special occasions or to share with others at Thanksgiving or Christmas time!

Nowadays when the weather is cold and dreary, I think about Great Aunt Janice's dumplings! They were simply delicious, and to this day, I haven't had any dumplings to come close to tasting like hers.

I remember when it would be burning hot down in the country in the summertime, Great Aunt Janice would leave the parlor, walk over to the Great Grandmother's cabinet, and get one of those BIG thick old *glasses and pour in some hot coffee with a little milk, sugar, sometimes a tiny spirit, and large chunks of ice from the icebox from the side porch! Homemade iced coffee! I had never seen anyone mix ingredients like that before for consumption! Rest assured, today, I drink iced coffee in the summertime – not just as a memory of Great Aunt Janice – but because iced coffee is delicious on a hot day! Whew!!*

Despite the fact that Great Aunt Janice didn't have much, she was awfully fashionable and professional in her attire! Just know that back in the day she knew how to accessorize and Great Auntie Janice could hang either one of her simple or pinstripe black or navy blue suits on any given day. She could hook up any outfit with a plain chalk-white blouse, one of her three large rhinestone brooches, medium or small button earrings, and drape clenched teeth foxes around herself. She could have pearls around her neck and wear a Madame Walker pressed and pulled back hairdo – an every strand in place, small hairbun tucked neat and tightly fixed in place. She could sport one of her three hats with veil over eye, showcasing all of her natural beauty without vanity. She had a strut that Betty Davis, Joan Crawford,

Naomi Campbell or any woman alive today would envy! Great Aunt Janice loved her dog, Brownie, a mixed Belgian Shepherd. She loved Spam & Jack, Great Grandmother's & Great Granddaddy's dogs, down in the country in Virginia. She loved to sing, dance, and cut up at times. She smoked Chesterfield cigarettes and drank Age & Age whiskey! Just know, she never smoked in public because it wasn't ladylike then! Great Aunt Janice loved to play cards, and she taught me how to play several card games. The first card game I ever learned was Solitaire, which I play online, daily. I recall times when Great Aunt Janice and Uncle Palmer would take a break away from the business and drive to one of the many juke joints in Southern Maryland. These joints had slot machines, sawdust dance floors, people dancing and having fun throughout the joint, a jukebox, and live bands too! Upon their arrival, sometimes, I would pop up from having stowed myself away in the back seat of the hearse. They would be mad!! My friend, Imelda, who lived at the corner would hide and ride with me. Great Aunt Janice and Uncle Palmer would be upset for a spell, but they wouldn't stay mad long because they were ready to relax and party too with their friends! As you know, during those days, children could go and pop up anywhere with adults in juke joints, and it was okay! I always felt happy and safe with Great Aunt Janice and Uncle Palmer. They protected me in every regard! But one day, I got in BIG trouble with them when I ignored their instructions, and I got locked in the morgue for several hours with six dead bodies! Yikes!! That's another story for another family activity!

In closing, with all of the memories I hold close in my heart today of spending summers and other days with Great Aunt Janice and Uncle Palmer down in the country, at their funeral home, or anywhere until I was grown, are the memories that extend to my brothers, Dickie and Kenny Boy. Great Aunt Janice shared her culinary experiences and poured love on them too, specifically on Saturdays and Sundays after choir practice and church activities. Amazingly, I can't for the life of me remember when my beloved Great Aunt Janice passed from this life. I believe that I just blocked it out of mind because I miss her so much! I certainly remember the day her sister, your mother – my grandmother – passed through this world. Gladys Powell left us on the evening of June 9, 1975, at 5:55 p.m. I was right there in the room when *she transitioned, as Uncle Jimmy, your brother, was bringing her dinner upstairs! As I pondered from time to time, I believe Great Aunt Janice's birthday was June 23rd, and her death year was 1977. Nevertheless, Great Aunt Janice's spirit lives on with me forever!! I will always treasure her memory and miss her all the days of my life because she treated me well – princess-like – with much love, respect, and she took excellent care of me whenever I was sick or in good health!*

My beloved Aunt Frankie, I hope this helps you with your planning and preparation to hold your event that will go down in my mind and be remembered as "Aunt Frankie's Family Affair." The event is scheduled for Saturday, April 18, 2020 at 1:00 p.m., at 11708 Hickory Drive, Fort Washington, Maryland 20744! I am looking forward to seeing you then. I have started working on the paper you asked me to prepare specific to "The Importance of Your Heritage" presentation. I can assure you it won't be long. Also, I believe it is a good idea for me to prepare a few questions for you to ask family members about our heritage – particularly the young folks so that they can at least know who they are celebrating during the family event. It'll be your call to take a look at my paper and the questions before I present it! In the meantime, take care of yourself. Exhale often, relax, and enjoy your day. I am. I wrote all of these wonderful things about Great Aunt Janice. Just know, that I love and adore you too. See you soon, and thank you for planning this activity for our family. I love you! Smooches.

Pictures

www.ingramcontent.com/pod-product-compliance
Lightning Source LLC
LaVergne TN
LVHW021958060526
838201LV00048B/1612